MATERIALS, PROCESS, PRINT.

Southampton
SOLENT

Published in 2007 by
Laurence King Publishing Ltd
361–373 City Road
London EC1V 1LR
United Kingdom

T: +44 20 7841 6900
F: +44 20 7841 6910
E-mail: enquiries@laurenceking.co.uk
www.laurenceking.co.uk

A catalogue record for this book is
available from the British Library.

ISBN–10: 1 85669 510 7
ISBN–13: 978 1 85669 510 7

Design and art direction by
Saturday-London.

Printed in China.

MATERIALS, PROCESS, PRINT.

CREATIVE SOLUTIONS FOR GRAPHIC DESIGN

Daniel Mason
Print Case Studies by Angharad Lewis,
Daniel Mason and Caroline Roberts

Laurence King Publishing

INTRODUCTION

This handbook is both a visual reference and a guide to a selection of commonly available materials and manufacturing processes for designers and for individuals tasked with commissioning design. The majority of these substrates and manufacturing methods have been used for conventional ends, but have never really been examined in great detail for what they are, as opposed to their function in any given print project. That is the intention of this book.

The second half of the book is a selection of case studies in which a designer has considered the materials and manufacturing processes themselves as being key to the execution of the project. The book also examines what could be achieved if one were to stretch to the limit the possibilities that the substrates and manufacturing methods offer.

Common problems faced when considering the introduction of alternative processes and materials to a project are restraints of budget and time. Print manufacture has become highly commodified, and there is now a plethora of companies that can offer competitive prices and short delivery times. Printing is a service-led business where the focus today is not on what is being produced, but more on the customers' satisfaction with the service. This commodification leads to a limited choice of printing stocks, formats, manufacturing methods and finishing; this is a state of affairs that does not allow a more expansive viewpoint for the creative process, and can be highly restrictive when producing an idea in multiples.

This 'dumbing down' of printing has led to a belief that if something isn't printed on ordinary paper then it must cost a lot more to produce, and take more time. Strictly speaking this is probably true, but it means that the expectation threshold has been lowered so much that it is becoming increasingly difficult for the designer, client and customer to overreach their expectations, to challenge what they know and to produce work that may be of a greater aesthetic value.

If you arm yourself with as much information as possible to present to both client and supplier, then any project you undertake may be able to utilize some of the ideas described in this book. It all comes down to the constant collation of information. Part of this information-gathering process is the establishment of the time it will take to produce this type of work. This will require some research. It is also important never to be overly swayed by the excitement of discovering something that has never been attempted before. It may be all right to ask if a material is available in other colours, but you have to be aware of how long these will take to deliver and what other processes may also be involved that could impede their use.

Information, then, operates on a number of levels: as a guide to the client it provides assurance in trying alternatives, while to the designer it gives confidence when approaching the supplier to attempt something new, and it also allows them to build up an impressive level of manufacturing knowledge.

In fact, confidence has a major part to play in this information-gathering process. The fear of the unknown can often make designers reticent about proposing a new substrate or manufacturing method. It is a case of being deliberate and conscientious about sourcing suppliers and building a relationship with them. The supplier holds the knowledge.

A strong relationship will allow you to begin to experiment with or utilize a production method. You need to visit factories, stand on the shop floor and see how things are printed. Speaking to machine minders and finishers can tell you far more than relying on a sales brochure, specification sheet or salesperson. Dialogue with peers can also assist in building your confidence—their previous experience can help resolve present issues, though shared information about the best suppliers may not be as forthcoming. Neither should you rely on the advertisements in design magazines. A much better source of information is trade literature, where all the data will be assessed for practical and not inspirational needs.

The computer shares some of the blame as to why the design process has become such a linear pursuit. Clients demand work for approval immediately, and with the exponential leaps in technology it is easy to satisfy this demand. What exists on screen is what the client expects to receive. This does not allow for any variables and the amendments can be made digitally. Nothing is left to chance. The computer has created a direct route, without variation, from the screen in the studio to the cardboard box in which the finished work is delivered.

It is difficult to break from this way of working. If at all possible a new working method needs to be established whereby you can be allowed to test ideas about these materials and processes both for presentation and to show the client that you are expanding your thoughts about their projects. It will also require an alternative method of communicating what you wish to achieve, being proactive about increasing the value of their communications material and making it more exciting to see, touch and perhaps even smell.

You will have to factor in the possibility that things may go wrong or may not appear as you intended. In the absence of prior experimentation it may well not be possible to manage expectations. A great number of questions need to be asked before a project goes into production. Potential problems need to be ironed out with your supplier. Hopefully, what is outlined in this book will ensure that you know what kinds of problems might arise.

Knowledge of materials and processes should enable you to collate a notional set of scenarios that can be presented to a supplier, allowing the possibility of experimentation to run in tandem with other work. If you come across a material sample, see if you can get it printed up without inconveniencing the running of a factory. These experiments may not have an immediate application but should be retained for future use. Time should be set aside to discuss these ideas if there is to be any commitment to seeing them happen.

What about the question of how to store all these data and samples? There is no simple answer. Unless your company has personnel to handle all the data it is probably better to dispose of the majority of the samples gathered when a project is finished and start collecting again when work begins on a new project. If you retain what appeals and discard the rest as an ongoing process, a bespoke archive of materials and processes will begin to develop.

Some materials and processes possess their own hidden importance and meaning. The transposition of manufacturing methods or materials from one industry to another can imbue your project with other layers of meaning and can create another history. For example, if the project needs to look and feel industrial then why not employ materials and processes that are drawn from these fields? This may give your work an added dimension of authenticity.

It must also be pointed out that some of these materials and processes have to be more cost-effective than more conventionally understood manufacturing methods. Packaging, for instance, for foodstuffs or hardware items forms a negligible cost component compared to the overall cost of such product; so it is cheaper than putting something in a box or a bag. However, one must be mindful that the processes may require high volumes to achieve these costs. In the smaller runs of bespoke print or packaging, similar—and seemingly standard—packaging could prove far from viable.

You also have to remember that some of the more industrial-type processes or materials are intended for markets beyond the aesthetic world of design. This means that the personnel involved in these industries may have no knowledge or understanding of your requirements. They may also talk in a language that has no relevance to your objectives. In the majority of instances you will not be able to alter what is on offer to achieve your own ends. This will only cause frustration on both sides. However, if you persevere, this is another form of experimentation that may be more time-consuming but can yield innovative results. This kind of experimentation can often be inspirational and may push projects down routes that lead to unanticipated outcomes.

Finally, it should be noted that all the mentions of lithography in this book refer to sheet-fed offset lithography unless specifically mentioned. In addition, some of the materials and process terms may appear to be general—rigid PVC or binding, for instance. This is aimed at establishing a quick route map into the substrates and techniques discussed.

MATERIALS

INTRODUCTION

INTRODUCTION

The choice of materials described on the following pages has been based on a number of factors. Firstly, most of these materials are commonly available from a variety of merchants and there should be no particular challenge in finding them. The entries do, however, offer some ideas of what else could be available, given the opportunity of sourcing it. Most materials are produced by a company and sold by a merchant, but it is common for the merchants to be selective in the range they stock. For instance, they may well offer a stunning selection of colours but only one weight. Sometimes merchants may also rename products and colours, causing a great deal of confusion.

Most of these materials are used regularly in everyday life. You may encounter many of them throughout the day—getting up in the morning, doing your job or returning home at night. Some of these materials are instantly familiar, yet you may know little about their background, their history or their range of application. Such information should assist in empowering you to employ these materials; at the least it should help to fill a gap in your knowledge of them.

Conventional print processes can be employed on most of the materials selected here without too many manufacturing problems. For instance, if you have never printed on plastic before, you might predict a myriad of production issues, but these can all be resolved, given time and patience. All materials can be experimented with, but it will take time and organization to ensure that these experiments work.

The selection avoids reviewing materials that are too wayward or unusual. From experience, their supply is highly fragmented and their cost is often beyond the budget of a given project. Unusual substrates have normally been produced for one specific job and no other. Sometimes they can be very attractive to look at but are impossible to print or convert. In other instances they are only available in one colour, and that colour rarely seems to be the one you want.

Materials are generally seen as falling into two categories—synthetic and non-synthetic. One should not scrutinize these categories too closely, but they do serve as a useful division in the selection of substrates, when the demands of a project require rapid choices to be made in specifying one material over another. Although this can usefully act as a first level in the selection process, further research will often reveal different shades, colours and finishes that may swiftly break down the synthetic/non-synthetic divide. However, this can allow for the subversion of expectation, and also for the use of materials that masquerade as something that they are not—a synthetic paper, or a flexible PVC that looks like wood, for example.

A major problem is that many manufacturers fail to produce samples or effective literature on products. They often claim that materials will print easily and finish in a number of ways. The reality is that they will not, and the printer or finisher is unwilling to spend the extra time required to make it work. The designer often needs to take on the role of the conduit between manufacturer and printer, and has to face the reality of a material's limitations, despite ignorance of the problems at hand. This ignorance, however, can lead to unique results. A lack of full awareness of a material's capacities forces it to be pushed or applied in new directions, and this can be when genuine innovation occurs.

ACRYLIC

Acrylic can be supplied in a wide range of colours, sizes and thicknesses, though sometimes not directly from stock. Acrylic usually has a highly glossy surface and can be prone to scratching. This is why it is always supplied with a protective film on both sides of the material. It is available in the form of cast or extruded acrylic sheet. Cast acrylic sheet is produced directly between two sheets of glass. It is more rigid than extruded acrylic, easier to cut and glue, and available in a wider variety of colours and finishes. Extruded acrylic is made from granules of plastic and is thus the preferred material for thermoforming, a process in which the sheet is heated until pliable, then draped over a male mould and allowed to cool, taking on the mould's shape.

Acrylic can be cut with a saw. Once it has been sawn, the edges can be flame polished, which will leave a gloss finish. However, if you are intending to print on the acrylic, you need to be aware that flame polishing the edges can have an effect on the surrounding flat surface, causing any print to crack and craze. Acrylic can also be glued, though only specific adhesives that are

highly watery in consistency can be used. The material can also be softened on a wire and heat bent into angles. Heat bending can also cause acrylic to flare out at the bend. This is difficult to avoid, particularly when the item is being mass produced, and is uneconomical to rectify.

In terms of the surface of the acrylic, foil blocking can be applied. The surface can also be engraved; this can be attractive but is often costly and time-consuming. Screen printing a translucent white has the same effect as engraving and can be a cheaper alternative.

Glow-edge acrylic is one of the more unusual materials available. There are chemicals inside the sheet that emit a bright glow when light hits the material. The colour palette and thicknesses available are restricted (for example, lime green, yellow, orange and blue), but there is a sheet available in a 0.3mm thickness, which is suitable for business cards and invitations, and which has the additional advantage that it can be guillotined.

See *Noting Absence* — Anna Blessmann and Peter Saville [pp.062–064]

THE GOSPEL ACCORDING TO
ST. JOHN

CHAPTER 1

√ the beginning was the Word, and the Word was with God, and the Word was God.

he same was in the beginning with God.

All things were made by him; and with-t him was not any thing made that was de.

n him was life; and the life was the light men.

And the light shineth in darkness; and e darkness comprehended it not.

There was a man sent from God, whose me was John.

The same came for a witness, to bear tness of the Light, that all men through n might believe.

He was not that Light, but was sent to ar witness of that Light.

That was the true Light, which lighteth ery man that cometh into the world.

He was in the world, and the world was de by him, and the world knew him not.

He came unto his own, and his own ceived him not.

But as many as received him, to them ve he power to become the sons of God, en to them that believe on his name:

Which were born, not of blood, nor of e will of the flesh, nor of the will of man, it of God.

And the Word was made flesh, and dwelt nong us, (and we beheld his glory, the ory as of the only begotten of the Fa-er,) full of grace and truth.

¶ John bare witness of him, and cried, ying, This was he of whom I spake, He at cometh after me is preferred before e: for he was before me.

And of his fulness have all we received, d grace for grace.

For the law was given by Moses, but ace and truth came by Jesus Christ.

No man hath seen God at any time; the ly begotten Son, which is in the bosom the Father, he hath declared him.

¶ And this is the record of John, when e Jews sent priests and Levites from Jeru-lem to ask him, Who art thou?

And he confessed, and denied not; but nfessed, I am not the Christ.

And they asked him, What then? Art ou Elias? And he saith, I am not. Art ou that prophet? And he answered, No.

Then said they unto him, Who art thou? at we may give an answer to them that nt us. What sayest thou of thyself?

He said, I am the voice of one crying in e wilderness, Make straight the way of

25 And they asked him, and said unto him, Why baptizest thou then, if thou be not that Christ, nor Elias, neither that prophet?

26 John answered them, saying, I baptize with water: but there standeth one a-mong you, whom ye know not;

27 He it is, who coming after me is pre-ferred before me, whose shoe's latchet I am not worthy to unloose.

28 These things were done in Bethabara beyond Jordan, where John was baptizing.

29 ¶ The next day John seeth Jesus coming unto him, and saith, Behold the Lamb of God, which taketh away the sin of the world.

30 This is he of whom I said, After me cometh a man which is preferred before me: for he was before me.

31 And I knew him not: but that he should be made manifest to Israel, therefore am I come baptizing with water.

32 And John bare record, saying, I saw the Spirit descending from heaven like a dove, and it abode upon him.

33 And I knew him not: but he that sent me to baptize with water, the same said unto me, Upon whom thou shalt see the Spirit descending, and remaining on him, the same is he which baptizeth with the Holy Ghost.

34 And I saw, and bare record that this is the Son of God.

35 ¶ Again the next day after John stood, and two of his disciples;

36 And looking upon Jesus as he walked, he saith, Behold the Lamb of God!

37 And the two disciples heard him speak, and they followed Jesus.

38 Then Jesus turned, and saw them fol-lowing, and saith unto them, What seek ye? They said unto him, Rabbi, (which is to say, being interpreted, Master,) where dwellest thou?

39 He saith unto them, Come and see. They came and saw where he dwelt, and abode with him that day: for it was about the tenth hour.

40 One of the two which heard John speak, and followed him, was Andrew, Simon Peter's brother.

41 He first findeth his own brother Simon, and saith unto him, We have found the Messias, which is, being interpreted, the Christ.

42 And he brought him to Jesus. And when Jesus beheld him, he said, Thou art Simon the son of Jona: thou shalt be called Cephas, which is by interpretation, A stone.

43 ¶ The day following Jesus would go forth into Galilee, and findeth Philip, and

Christ turns water into wine · He purges the temple

45 Philip findeth Nathanael, and saith un-to him, We have found him, of whom Moses in the law, and the prophets, did write, Jesus of Nazareth, the son of Joseph.

46 And Nathanael said unto him, Can there any good thing come out of Na-zareth? Philip saith unto him, Come and see.

47 Jesus saw Nathanael coming to him, and saith of him, Behold an Israelite indeed, in whom is no guile!

48 Nathanael saith unto him, Whence knowest thou me? Jesus answered and said unto him, Before that Philip called thee, when thou wast under the fig tree, I saw thee.

49 Nathanael answered and saith unto him, Rabbi, thou art the Son of God; thou art the King of Israel.

50 Jesus answered and said unto him, Be-cause I said unto thee, I saw thee under the fig tree, believest thou? thou shalt see greater things than these.

51 And he saith unto him, Verily, verily, I say unto you, Hereafter ye shall see hea-ven open, and the angels of God ascending and descending upon the Son of man.

CHAPTER 2

AND the third day there was a marriage in Cana of Galilee; and the mother of Jesus was there:

2 And both Jesus was called, and his dis-ciples, to the marriage.

3 And when they wanted wine, the mother of Jesus saith unto him, They have no wine.

4 Jesus saith unto her, Woman, what have I to do with thee? mine hour is not yet come.

5 His mother saith unto the servants, Whatsoever he saith unto you, do it.

6 And there were set there six waterpots of stone, after the manner of the purifying of the Jews, containing two or three firkins apiece.

7 Jesus saith unto them, Fill the waterpots with water. And they filled them up to the brim.

8 And he saith unto them, Draw out now, and bear unto the governor of the feast. And they bare it.

9 When the ruler of the feast had tasted the water that was made wine, and knew not whence it was: (but the servants which drew the water knew;) the governor of the feast called the bridegroom,

10 And saith unto him, Every man at the beginning doth set forth good wine; and when men have well drunk, then that which is worse: but thou hast kept the good wine until now.

11 This beginning of miracles did Jesus in Cana of Galilee, and manifested forth his glory; and his disciples believed on him.

12 ¶ After this he went down to Caper-

ST. JOHN 2

13 ¶ And the Jews' passover was at ha and Jesus went up to Jerusalem,

14 And found in the temple those t sold oxen and sheep and doves, and changers of money sitting:

15 And when he had made a scourge small cords, he drove them all out of temple, and the sheep, and the oxen; a poured out the changers' money, and ov threw the tables;

16 And said unto them that sold dow Take these things hence; make not Father's house an house of merchandis

17 And his disciples remembered that was written, The zeal of thine house h eaten me up.

18 ¶ Then answered the Jews and said to him, What sign shewest thou unto seeing that thou doest these things?

19 Jesus answered and said unto the Destroy this temple, and in three day will raise it up.

20 Then said the Jews, Forty and six ye was this temple in building, and wilt th rear it up in three days?

21 But he spake of the temple of his boo

22 When therefore he was risen from dead, his disciples remembered that had said this unto them; and they believ the scripture, and the word which Je had said.

23 ¶ Now when he was in Jerusalem at passover, in the feast day, many belie in his name, when they saw the mirac which he did.

24 But Jesus did not commit himself u them, because he knew all men,

25 And needed not that any should tes of man: for he knew what was in man.

CHAPTER 3

THERE was a man of the Pharise named Nicodemus, a ruler of Jews:

2 The same came to Jesus by night, a said unto him, Rabbi, we know that th art a teacher come from God: for no n can do these miracles that thou do except God be with him.

3 Jesus answered and said unto him, Ver verily, I say unto thee, Except a man born again, he cannot see the kingdom God.

4 Nicodemus saith unto him, How ca man be born when he is old? can he en the second time into his mother's wor and be born?

5 Jesus answered, Verily, verily, I say to thee, Except a man be born of wa and of the Spirit, he cannot enter into kingdom of God.

6 That which is born of the flesh is fle and that which is born of the Spirit spirit.

BIBLE PAPER

Bible paper is an extremely thin printing paper, and has been made from a wide variety of materials, from rags to wood pulp. Its lightness belies the fact that the material is exceptionally strong and retains a reasonable degree of opacity.

The first person to consider using it for printing was Thomas Combe, printer to the University of Oxford, who discovered it in use in the kilns of the Staffordshire potteries and was impressed by its high tensile strength and its flexibility. This 'India paper' was originally made from recycled ships' ropes, and was used from 1875 for printing bibles and prayer books, which could be con-densed into very small volumes for the first time.

Today, as 'bible paper', it is usually made from wood pulp and is also employed for other text-heavy tomes, such as dictionaries and encyclopaedias. The printing of all such volumes is highly specialized, and presses are dedicated to their sole production. The introduction of bible paper into the commercial print environment can cause problems, as the paper has the tendency to stretch and curl as a result of its thinness. Bible paper also tends to cockle when solid areas of ink are printed, so it is advisable to run the sheets through the machine very slowly.

Bible paper foil blocks very well but care needs to be taken because of its lightness. However, the strength of the paper allows it to be creased and folded many times without the print cracking.

Despite being available in just one thickness, bible paper's off-white colour, together with its elasticity and thinness, all conspire to make it unique, constrained by certain limitations but liberated by others.

BOOK CLOTH

Book cloth is a woven cotton that is coated in a starch and pigment mixture that has been subjected to live steam before being spread across the cloth. The granules of starch burst open and thicken, causing the material to stiffen, giving the starched effect. Drying is usually done by a steam-heated drum, around which the cloth is wrapped during its journey through the spreading machine. The heat dries the starch on to the cloth. When the material is glued, the process is reversed as water in the glue softens the starch granules, making the material pliable and easy to work with. The starch prevents this glue from penetrating through the cloth.

Books had originally been bound in animal hides and papyrus, but both materials were costly and difficult to work with. An animal hide was an irregular shape with a number of imperfections. With the onset of mass printing and greater literacy by the middle of the nineteenth century, the demand for books intensified, and these materials could not cater for what had once been the preserve of the rich. Cloth was cheaper and could also be supplied on the reel, so it was more efficient to use.

It is more common to find paper-backed or tissue-lined book cloths on the market. These differ from cotton book cloths as their material is predominantly from a synthetic source, such as rayon. Cotton book cloth has the disadvantage that adhesive will penetrate the cloth when glued. Rayon has a flexible backing or lining that prevents this, and is also cheaper than cotton. A further advantage is the availability of much brighter colours and more variances of weave. Cotton book cloth tends to be associated with dry legal or medical tomes, while rayon cloth tends to be used for more art or design-based projects. Cotton cloth is also more durable than rayon.

As the world moves to other ways of consuming knowledge, use of book cloth is likely to decline. Even so, there is still a great variety of book cloths available, and it is the subject of ongoing research. Because of its international availability, there are manufacturers who supply book cloth on a global scale.

The 1950s saw the introduction and rise of coated papers, which could be coloured and embossed in all manner of finishes, some even mimicking animal hides. Animal skin finally had its revenge—if in a synthetic form. Now hybrid cloths have been created that fuse texture and weave, as well as replicating the finish of surfaces found in nature (stones) or science (metals and crystals). Manufacturers of these materials are more than willing to supply sumptuous swatch folders, but do exercise some caution—the world of book cloth is diverse, and the variety can prove dangerously hypnotic.

See *The Elusive Truth!* — Jason Beard [pp.065–067]

COLOURED PAPER

The majority of, if not all, coloured papers that are commercially available are supplied uncoated. The choice of colours and weights is fairly broad, but, as so few mills continue its production, one tends to find the same shades and qualities available everywhere—continued research to uncover interesting alternatives is often a fruitless task.

Coloured paper can also be supplied with a range of embossed textures on one side of the material. These finishes are currently in high demand for use in packaging, report covers and stationery.

Commercially available weights of coloured paper range from around 100gsm moving up to 350gsm. For a thicker material, sheets have to be bonded together or duplexed. This is very effective but can make the material prohibitively expensive. You could consider the option of printing a colour on to a board of the required thickness, though the edges of the board will not be coloured.

Coloured paper lends itself well to all printing processes—screen printing and foil blocking are particularly effective. With black papers that have a high carbon content, there can be an adverse reaction to foil blocking—this can affect the appearance of the foil. Coloured paper die cuts and creases well, and therefore can be a good choice for the construction of cartons if a luxury finish is required. However, as the material is usually supplied uncoated, it is soft, making the board liable to delaminate on flaps and closures.

You may find it interesting to obtain samples of the more unusual colours or shades that are available, even if you might not have any immediate intention of using them. Also, where possible, experiment with ink colours and foil blocking as unintended results may yield new creative possibilities.

See Makri jewellery packaging — Spin [pp.077–079]

CORK

Simply, cork is the bark of the cork tree. In spring and summer the bark is easily removed from the trees. Cork trees have to be fully grown for this to be possible. Consequently an investment of a considerable period of time is required to allow the trees to be nurtured for constant harvesting.

Cork has been used throughout history, but the biggest step forward for the industry was its use as a replacement for wooden stoppers wrapped in hemp and soaked in olive oil in the bottling of champagne. Commercial cork production for wine started in the 1750s, with the waste being converted into materials such as cork-and-rubber composite, which has industrial uses.

Cork is extremely buoyant, as more than 50 per cent of its structure is air, yet it remains solid. Because of this, it remains very compressible without breaking, making it flexible and resilient. This is why it is used for such diverse roles as flooring and even in the nose cone of the space shuttle. It is easy to silk-screen; however, with the

natural surface being randomly uneven, finish can be problematical, particularly when attempting to print fine text or complicated logos. Cork can also be die cut and guillotined with comparative ease.

Researchers are investigating the possibility that cork could be injection moulded or thermoformed, though the research is still in its infancy. Currently, availability of this material tends to be restricted to cork tiles, which are on sale at DIY and craft outlets. Also worth investigating are cork-and-rubber composite materials, which tend to be found anywhere where industrial flooring is sold. In addition, there are cork bale-binding cloths available, which could have packaging applications.

The application of cork could be seen as limited, but its uneven surface and cellular structure, coupled with the various tints available as a tile, could make this material an alternative option for a project. If not, it would make a worthy inclusion within the palette of surface textures and materials for presentation to a client.

CORRUGATED CARDBOARD

Corrugated cardboard consists of flat outer sheets, or liners, of puncture-resistant paper, sandwiching a central core or filling of corrugated fluted paper (called a medium) that resists crushing under compression. When used in a box this gives cushioning and protection to the box's contents. The liner and medium are glued together along the outsides of the peaks and valleys of each flute. The cardboard has high end-to-end strength along the corrugated flutes, so boxes are normally designed with the flutes running vertically for stacking strength.

Common flute sizes are A, B, C, E and F or, at the smallest extreme, micro flute. This letter designation relates to the order in which the flutes were invented, not their relative sizes. Flute size refers to the number of flutes per lineal foot, with A being the least and biggest. Corrugated cardboard is commonly supplied with either white both sides or brown both sides, though the availability of brown corrugated card in thinner flutes from stock is becoming ever more limited.

In addition, double- and triple-wall corrugated boards are manufactured for specialized industrial applications.

Micro-flute is manufactured for fine-printed packaging, when a printed sheet is laminated to the material. It is important to exercise caution when die cutting or creasing this laminated material, as it has a tendency to crack the print. It can be screen printed and flexo printed. It could also be foil blocked, although the process is not ideally suited to this material.

Corrugated cardboard is manufactured using high-precision machinery lines called corrugators. Various types of converting machinery are used to manufacture boxes from the board that comes off the corrugator. For example, the flexo-folder gluer is a machine that, in one single pass, prints, cuts, folds and glues flat sheets of board to convert them to boxes for any application. Much corrugated packaging relies on staples and glue to hold it together. However, experimentation through cardboard engineering can reveal some other methods that do not rely on this element of the finishing process. The perfect example of this is the hinged-lid transit box.

See Damien Hirst print transit box [pp.092–094]

FELT

Felt is made from wool matted together into fabric by beating, rolling, suction and pressure. The most common type of wool used in the manufacture of felt is sheep wool—this works well because each fibre is hollow in construction with overlapping scales on the outside of each filament. When wet, these scales swell and open up slightly. As these wool fibres touch each other, the swollen scales interlock and become entangled—the non-woven matrix that results is known as felt.

The wool fibres are extensively cleaned and blown through to a large holding vat. The blowing action serves to mix the wool fibres together. At this stage other fibres can be introduced into the mix to achieve certain properties or alter the look of the felt. The blended wool is then placed into carding machines that draw the wool fibre out on large rotating combs. This process layers these fibres to produce a pre-felted sheet of fabric.

These sheets are layered together under two large canvas-lined plates, which come together and compress the material. Steam is forced between the plates to make the scales of the wool fibre swell. The plates then rotate in opposite directions, causing the fibres to interlock. Thus the felting process begins. The longer it remains between these two plates the thinner the felt will become. All that is required is for it to be dried. The drying process stabilizes the fabric and sets both the thickness and the width. The felt is placed on a conveyer belt where it is kept taut by hooks holding on to the belt.

Some felts can be dyed in a variety of colours. Felt is available direct from the manufacturer, but the brighter colours tend to be for the handicraft market—the largest palette tends to be supplied to a thickness of 1mm. It is rare that you will come across thicker felts in any colours other than black. This is partly because you cannot dye the felt consistently. A more limited palette of colours, but one with a far more interesting texture, is provided by 'industrial' felts. Usually supplied in off-white, grey and brown, this felt type is used to polish and to finish jewellery and metalwork and can be found encasing the strikers of church bells. Industrial felt could be seen as having a texture and finish aligned to materials such as grey board and corrugated cardboard.

Printing methods tend to be restricted to screen printing, and it is difficult to achieve a fine print as the material is quite fibrous. Felt makes an interesting covering material and can be converted into dust jackets as an alternative to book cloth. It cannot easily be used as a covering material in rigid box making, however, as it cannot be glued.

See *Undercover Jun Takahashi Featured by W.W. —
Communion W* [pp.104–106]

FLEXIBLE PVC

Flexible PVC (polyvinyl chloride) is a variant of rigid PVC. The introduction of plasticizers to this substrate, first attempted in the 1920s, makes it more pliable. It was further developed during the Second World War, when it had military applications. Flexible PVC is now commonly used in the manufacture of stationery such as binders and holders for car-parking permits. Unlike rigid PVC, flexible PVC is available in an extremely large selection of colours and finishes. The stationery market, like fashion, is prone to trends, and manufacturers of flexible PVC produce tints and embossings to shadow shifts in taste.

The majority of suppliers have complex networks of agencies and merchants who sell the material. This means that what is found in one country is usually common to another. The colour and weight selection is very broad, encompassing day-glo tints right through to black, and, like coloured paper, it is available in a number of embossed finishes. Flexible PVC should be used with care as each version has a very specific use or application, and it can react to any print that it comes into contact with. It has a tendency to lift print off surfaces—the print often attaches itself, like a transfer, to this substrate. This occurs because of the high proportion of plasticizer in flexible PVC's make-up.

Flexible PVC can be screen printed, and some grades can be printed lithographically. It debosses very well when high-frequency welded, a process which is ideally suited to this substrate. It is also worth considering as an alternative material for invitations, for example.

Flexible PVC is supplied on reels and is notoriously difficult to convert into flat sheets. This is because suppliers normally ship to factories that use it straight from the reel. These manufacturers can cut it for you, but they will normally insist that they also print your job. In most instances, however, such manufacturers will not pay the same attention to detail as a specialist or screen printer. Please note that specific inks are required for printing on flexible PVC. In addition, it is not possible to print then deboss in register, as the high-frequency welding process will lift the ink.

It would be worthwhile researching more unusual and non-presentation versions of flexible PVC. For instance, a thin, black, embossed flexible PVC was found to be suitable for a coffin lining, while its white counterpart has been used to line a baby's pram. There is also a semi-translucent version that is used for blood bags, while thicknesses of up to 5mm are used for factory-door curtains. Flexible PVC is an invaluable substrate in your arsenal. It is well worth experimenting with, and also tracking its progress for new versions.

See *The Shadow of the Official Artworks —* Mo'design Inc. [pp.101–103]

GREY BOARD

Grey board is made from recycled waste paper, using a production process that is very energy intensive. Bales of waste paper are placed into a pulper—a steel cauldron filled with water, fitted with a rotor arm. The soaked waste paper then begins to break up, and the turbulence produced by the rotor arm mixes the fibres with the water, producing slurry.

This slurry is pumped into a head box, from which it is distributed on to an endless screen called a wire. It is in the first few metres of the wire that the board takes shape. The water disperses and the paper fibres remain behind and bind to each other. The wet board is squeezed between two presses where supporting felts soak up and remove more of the water. By this stage the board is becoming more rigid.

Finally, the board is then passed over steam-heated cylinders, causing most of the remaining water to evaporate. The resultant grey board is now ready to be used in its raw state or it can be sent off to be laminated, into display board for example.

Grey board has a wide variety of traditional uses. Because of its low cost and rigidity it is principally sold to make covers for hardback books, and forms the core material in high-frequency welded binders, files, diaries and even jigsaws. It is a material that tends not to be seen; a material that serves a purpose.

Despite being very rigid, grey board is still soft enough to be foil blocked, giving a debossed effect. Also, interesting results can be achieved by foil blocking with a clear foil. It can also be screen printed, though the board may need to be sealed as it is very porous. Another alternative is to screen print the image twice to ensure a good coverage of ink, though this can cause problems with registration. When it is matt laminated, grey board takes on an unusual appearance, as the lamination takes on all the imperfections in the surface of the board.

Care should be taken when creasing grey board as it tends to crack. Another potential problem is that grey board, which has a high water content, can warp if left in direct sunlight, as it continues to dry out. The board should always be left shrink wrapped until it is required.

Grey board is such a rough-looking material that it can be imbued with all manner of meanings. It feels recycled and looks industrial, with a look and feel of being distinctly unprocessed compared to paper, for example; this lends itself to projects requiring a grittier, industrial feel. In some cases, attempting to make it look beautiful through foil blocking can create an uneasy relationship between material and process. This unease only serves to maximize the end result.

See MoslBuddJewChristHinDao — Elternhaus [pp.107–109]

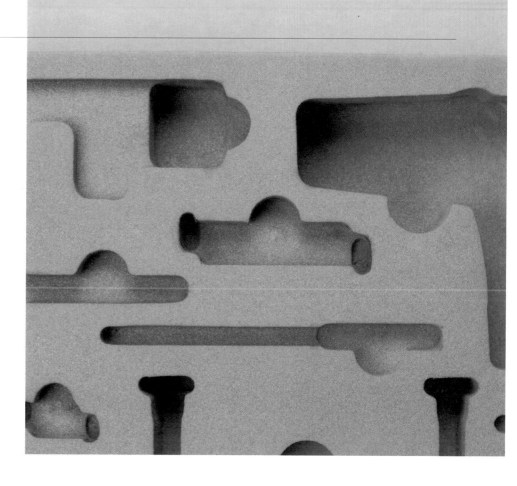

HIGH-DENSITY FOAM

High-density foam has a three-stage production process, commencing with polymer being blended in line and extruded into solid sheet or slab form. This sheet is then cross-linked to create a lattice-like structure at a molecular level within the material. This allows the material to be thermal moulded, as cross-linked foams can be stretched and compressed, and retain their shape when cooled.

High-density foam has a range of applications but can principally be employed by the designer as a packaging material to house a series of items securely and attractively without having to resort to over-engineered cardboard executions.

Typically these foams are supplied in buns or sheets with a manufacturing skin that makes the foam appear hard and shiny. Most fabrication operations require that the skin is removed from one or both faces and that the sheet is split to a specific thickness. This is the first stage of a sheet being made ready for production. It is worth enquiring with suppliers which sheet thicknesses are available, as splitting the sheets can be costly and you will probably wish to minimize the number of unsightly lamination lines.

It is possible for high-density foam trays to be form cut, but the material in the well of each aperture will have been cut all the way through, and if this happens it will then continually fall out. A better process is to rout the shapes, a process in which the coordinates of the design are computer programmed; a routing drill will then grind out all of the surplus material from the tray and form the required aperture.

High-density foam is commonly supplied in white and black, with colours having to be specially made. It may be worth checking with your supplier, who may have stocks left over from previous jobs. There are many grades of this material, some having been developed for very specific applications, for example as medical packaging, so you may have to modify your initial choices for budget reasons. It can be printed, but only very rudimentary results can be achieved.

It should be noted that, because of its cellular structure, high-density foam can expand and contract by as much as two per cent, depending on the ambient temperature of the room it is in. For this reason it should not be used if the required fit is very exact. This problem manifests itself most profoundly when it is being used as a tray in a rigid box. If the foam has contracted there will be a narrow gap around the perimeter of the tray; if it has expanded the foam block will no longer slide into the box.

Despite the problems described here, high-density foam is a very exciting material with great potential. It provides the designer with the ultimate alternative to conventional packaging materials, and it comes charged with interesting stories of and allusions to its medical and industrial heritage.

See Krink Ink — Alife [pp.110–112]

LEATHER

When selecting leather as a material, you face an almost infinite choice, particularly when considering its finish. It is a particularly expensive material to use, and subjective decisions based on expectations of how leather should feel and smell will normally lead you to the higher-priced skins.

Leather is mainly available at specialist merchants who usually supply skins to make accessories such as handbags and belts and have a language and pricing structure geared to manufacturers in this market. One alternative for designers looking for leather as a material is to visit fabric shops in the first instance to locate what you are looking for. Your choice may be restricted in these shops, but prices should be more reasonable.

The use of leather in the design and production of a project generally denotes wealth, tradition and luxury. Leather can be screen printed, embossed and foil blocked. However it should be noted that, because it is the skin

of an animal, the surface texture and thickness of leather varies, and this can hamper the application of a design. Care should also be taken when gluing as leather has a tendency to contract when mounted or bonded. More rigid leather will die cut and trim far better than softer pigskin or goatskin leather.

The range of colours readily available tends to be very basic, with the palette rarely deviating from brown, black or blue. Brighter colours tend to be dyed especially for clients' requirements. However you could find some material left over from someone else's order. Flooring leather also provides an extremely polished and rigid alternative to common conceptions of leather hides.

If cost is an issue there are a number of synthetic materials that mimic the grain of leather, and some have even been developed to smell like it too.

See Book Cloth — [p.014]

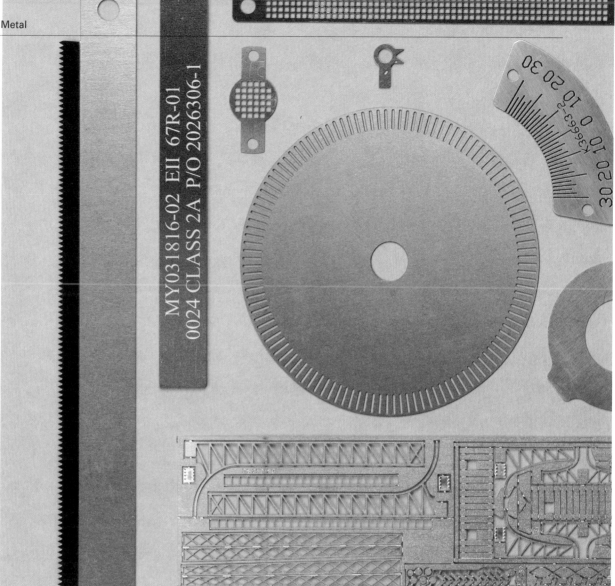

METAL

Along with some other materials discussed in this book, metal might be regarded as a substrate that has very few direct applications within the design process. It has a specific look, feel and density that will rarely be appropriate. However, if an application does arise, it is important to have some insight into what can be achieved, and how and where to get the project finished.

Cost is an important issue when considering using metal for a project, partly because, unlike papers or plastics, metal has to go through a number of processes prior to being ready to work with.

The metals most commonly used by designers are aluminium and stainless steel, both of which are easily cut, creased and screen printed. Stainless steel is much harder than aluminium and can be supplied in very thin gauges. However, the thinner the gauge the sharper the edges become. Stainless steel is particularly receptive to having designs etched into or through its surface.

Aluminium is lightweight and is a popular substrate for binders. Its edges do need to be sealed or anodized by immersing the material in an anodizing solution and running an electric current through it, otherwise it is prone to oxidization and marking from fingers.

There are not many suppliers and manufacturers who can produce high-quality finished goods from metal. The best place to start your research is to find suppliers who work within the architectural ironmongery field, or model makers and point-of-sale manufacturers. Make sure you factor in enough time for prototypes and production of the finished project in order to make the most of the material.

However, you may find that a great deal of effort is expended in utilizing this material only to conclude that mirri-board, for example, gives an equally satisfactory result. It is the hardness and the feel of metal that makes it an interesting material to use.

See *TG24, 24 Hours of Throbbing Gristle* and *TG+* — Peter Christopherson, Cosey Fanni Tutti, Chris Carter and Paul A. Taylor [pp.071–073]

MIRRI-BOARD

Mirri-board is manufactured by laminating thin films of metalized polyester to different base papers and boards. Its metallic and reflective surface lends itself principally to speciality packaging, such as perfume cartons, but the wide variety of colours and finishes available should allow you to specify its use for other applications.

There is also a range of holographic boards utilizing metalized polyester film that carries a micro-embossed holographic pattern. There is no choice beyond those patterns already available. Therefore any project that uses these materials has to be very specific in its requirements. The patterns also have 'shim lines'. These barely detectable lines occur where the pattern is butted up against itself and repeated. They are unavoidable and can create a grid over the finished work, which may be regarded as unsightly.

Despite their highly reflective and smooth surfaces, these materials can still be printed conventionally. With lithographic printing, inks must be selected that dry on non-absorbent substrates. UV-curable inks are also preferred. However, caution should be exercised with the more reflective boards when handling, as they have a tendency to scratch and mark. This laminated surface is soft, with any minor blemish being obvious to a naked eye because of the reflective mirror-quality appearance. With screen printing, inks must also be selected that will dry on non-absorbent surfaces. Certain inks need to cure for up to 48 hours, otherwise they will scratch.

Foil blocking and blind embossing both produce amazing results, and it is worth exploring different foil combinations on this stock. Overprinting mirri-board in translucent tints can also produce interesting results, particularly on more iridescent versions of the material.

See *What's Good?* book and DVD set —
AllRightsReserved Ltd [pp.119–121]

NEWSPRINT

Newsprint paper has to be strong and have a high opacity in its principal use for newspapers and comics. Traditionally it is used in web printing, where the paper is supplied and printed from a reel. Therefore it has to be able to run and print at high speed without tearing and marking.

Consequently the availability and specification of newsprint is very much geared towards these industries and its supply in sheet form is limited. In sheet form only one weight is supplied and this is usually found at most printers as an interleaving or packing material. Some screen printers print on sheet newsprint to dry out the ink in their screens. This can create some interesting, if uncontrolled, results on the work that is being produced.

Because of its lightness and tendency to absorb ink, newsprint can be difficult to print conventionally. The surface of newsprint is highly irregular because of its content—this comes predominantly from recycled sources, making it similar to grey board, and it performs like bible paper by curling and cockling when printed.

Newsprint can be supplied in a variety of weights, particularly at the lighter end of the scale, thanks to the demands of the market for the production of thinner substrates that will make newspaper publications lighter and thus more cost-effective to produce and ship. This requirement from the market for ever-lighter weights is making the heavier stocks harder to find.

Some designers may wish to produce a newspaper-style brochure. However, it may not be possible to use a conventional newspaper printer as production runs of newspapers are very high. It may be better to resort to a white or off-white thin uncoated paper to replicate the effect, and any four-colour work will also retain a level of sharpness and detail as a result.

Newsprint is still a valid material to consider in the arsenal of paper-based substrates that have an unusual handle and printed result without having to fall back on conventional coated and uncoated stocks. With adequate care and patience in printing and finishing, results can be achieved that make for idiosyncratic and desirable printed items.

See *Pura Seda Magazine* — Albert Folch Studio [pp.170–172]

PAPER

It is impossible to cover the broad subject of paper in any depth here. The focus of this section is on the properties of paper that need to be borne in mind when drawing up a specification—grammage, thickness and bulk. These three basic properties must be considered together as they are mathematically linked.

Grammage is usually given in weight per square metre and is a fundamental concept when choosing a paper. Grammage is often used to refer to a paper's thickness. This is misleading as thickness actually depends on a paper's bulk.

Thickness is measured in micrometres—thousandths of a millimetre—and is the distance between the paper's two surfaces. The thickness of the paper will affect the stability and feel of the final printed product.

Bulk, sometimes referred to as volume, defines the relationship between a paper's thickness and its grammage. A paper with a low bulk will be more compact and will contain less air than one with a high bulk. A low-bulk paper is thus thin and heavy, while a high-bulk paper is comparatively light, airy and thick. Because of the lower proportion of air, a low-bulk paper will often be smoother than one with a high bulk, and vice versa.

Roughness is another characteristic of paper to be considered. In general, uncoated papers have a higher roughness than coated papers. To reduce roughness the paper is compressed and smoothed in a calender or smoothing machine. There is a link between bulk and roughness, since a smooth, compressed paper will have a lower bulk. To achieve a higher bulk, the evenness of the paper surface will have to be compromised to some degree, and the paper will be rougher. Surface roughness may also affect the printing process, where more irregular, rougher papers can be difficult to print.

Opacity or non-translucency is another property of paper to consider. The higher a paper's opacity, the less translucent it is. A paper of 100 per cent opacity is therefore completely non-translucent, while one with a low opacity, such as tracing paper, is more translucent and lets a much higher proportion of light through. During printing, ink penetrates the paper and reduces its opacity, which can result in print being visible through the sheet. This is referred to as print opacity. This is an especially important consideration when double-sided printing, particularly on low grammage paper, and you need to be aware of the placement of text and graphics on both sides of the sheets.

The grain direction of a paper describes the orientation of the fibres that make up that sheet. This affects the stiffness of the paper and makes the paper harder to bend along that axis. Grain direction is also revealed by your paper supplier's measurements, as the figure given first refers to the length of the side that runs across the fibre direction.

POLYPROPYLENE

Polypropylene is an extremely common and widely used substrate across all areas of industry, products and design, largely because of its versatility, strength and resistance. As it is so widely employed, there are many variants available, depending on the process for which the material will be used.

Polypropylene is thought to have been discovered in the 1950s following research conducted within the polyethylene industry; but there is, as with most synthetic materials, some dispute as to who invented it first. Since its discovery, its use has grown exponentially.

Production of polypropylene utilizes a slurry, which is catalyzed through heat and pressure. These conditions are varied depending on the intended use of the product. The material does not present any cracking problems and can withstand very high temperatures. Its environmental impact is low thanks to the limited use of natural resources, low emissions, a long working life and optimal recycling capability. The only water used in its production, for instance, is in the cooling process, which is a closed operation, thus there is no external pollution of rivers and streams.

Sheet polypropylene comes in a broad variety of colours and thicknesses. The most commonly available sheets have a calendered, leather-like, embossed surface, probably because the material marks easily. The texture is also very waxy, which is off-putting to some designers. On the plus side, it screen prints well and can be printed more conventionally. In addition, it foil blocks and embosses without warping the finished sheet.

Unlike rigid PVC, polypropylene can be scored without snapping in two. It scores to leave a live hinge, but care should be taken to avoid cutting all the way through the material, because its density can vary across a sheet. Sheets of polypropylene can be welded together, which could be a better alternative to a locking tab when used for a box. It can also be riveted and stitched.

The popularity of polypropylene has been to the detriment of other materials. In the form of extruded film it is replacing cellophane, metal and even paper, as it is very resistant to being punctured. It is used for everything from caps and closures to garden furniture and toys. It is bright and durable, easily available and seen everywhere; and perhaps because of this ubiquity, it is not the first choice of the graphic designer, except when ring binders are required for presentations.

Even though polypropylene is widely marketed, the choice of solid opaque colours available from stock can be limited. It appears to promise so much, yet it seems that often only the ordinary is available. However, the white and clear sheets offer a greater range of weights and finishes. They also get closest to an industrial or scientific tone. Recycled polypropylene material, made from plastic bottles, is occasionally available. At present it is multi-coloured in finish, but plans are afoot to make it more colour specific. However, this will be reliant on the availability of recycled base material.

See Ryoji Ikeda, Mort aux Vaches Series — Angela Lorenz [pp.134–136]

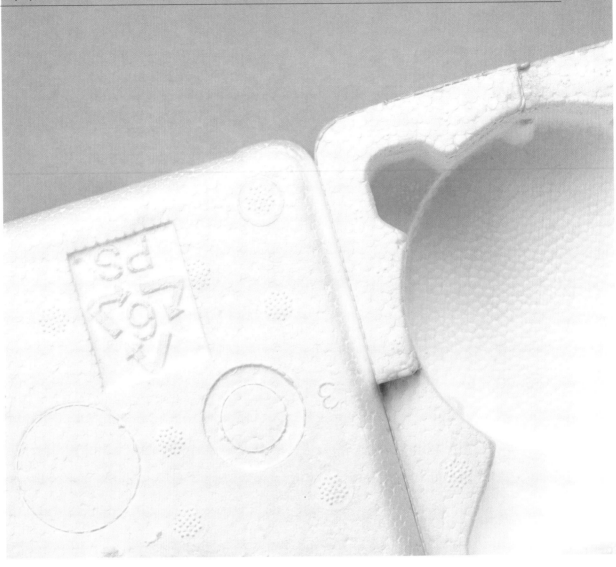

POLYSTYRENE

Polystyrene, commonly referred to as expanded polystyrene (EPS), has many applications from ceiling tiles through to transportation packaging and also its use as a building material. It does, however, remain largely unexplored for presentation applications.

The moulding of polystyrene is a three-part process called steam moulding. In the first stage tiny spherical EPS beads are expanded up to 40 times their original size. This expanding process is precisely timed to determine the size that the beads will finally reach. In this way different packaging products can be made to a required strength by increasing or decreasing the density.

In the second stage the beads are stored in huge canvas silos and are left to absorb air for 24 to 48 hours. Then, in stage three, the freshly expanded beads are poured into individually manufactured moulds where steam and pressure are applied, softening the beads and compressing them so that they bond together into the required shape and density. In a couple of minutes the formed item falls out of the mould.

A black variant of EPS exists that is used in thermo-insulation. The colour comes from introducing carbon flakes into the beads to enhance its thermal performance. This presents an attractive alternative to the commonly available white, but it contaminates the production line causing subsequent mouldings to become grey in colour. In addition there is a green variant, which is utilized for military applications.

Sheet polystyrene is moulded in large blocks that are cut using hot-wire cutting machines. These white sheets are commonly found in model shops. Some merchants are able to supply larger sheets with a greater choice of thickness. Sheet polystyrene is easily cut with a hot-wire foam cutter, which works by heating the wire to the point where it can vaporize the foam immediately adjacent to it. The foam is vaporized before actually touching the heated wire, which yields exceptionally smooth cuts. The cell structure of this material means that, in appearance, the material seems quite smooth; however, printing will achieve mixed results.

RIGID PVC

PVC (polyvinyl chloride) is one of the most commonly available and widely used of synthetic substrates. Because of this, it is one of the most valuable products of the petro-chemical industry. The majority of PVC is used in construction and heavy industries, but its ease of manufacture, and the huge number of variants that are available, make PVC a quick-fix choice for numerous applications beyond these industries.

PVC is in common use virtually everywhere. For example, in its rigid form it is used for credit cards, while in a slightly more flexible variant it is used for document wallets, which have a harder, drier feel than that of polypropylene, a material that is also commonly considered for such applications.

For use as a material for printing, PVC is normally supplied in white or clear sheets across a finite number of weights. There is a clear, mark-resistant version available; this has a calendered appearance, giving it the look of tracing paper.

Unlike polypropylene, PVC is not supplied from stock in a range of colours. From experience it can be very difficult to source particular shades without having to resort to having them specially made. This can be time-consuming, and the minimum orders often far outweigh your requirements. It is worth asking your supplier or printer if they can source what you want, but it is usually difficult for them to do so.

Virtually any printing process can be applied to rigid PVC. It offers a synthetic alternative to paper and is therefore used for anything from invitations, business cards, book covers and beyond. Rigid PVC is, however, expensive to print with, and the user has to be conscious of its limitations. For instance, as PVC is not regarded as environmentally friendly, it can be off-putting to both designer and client.

Caution has to be exercised when PVC is die cut as it has very sharp edges and the cut is not as smooth as with paper or board. Foil blocking and embossing can create particularly interesting results. However, PVC has a tendency to become uneven when these processes are applied to it.

See The Backpack Project poster — Juliette Cezzar [pp.143–145]

RUBBER

Rubber stimulates a number of senses, from touch to smell. Its history and manufacture are long and complicated, and the material itself is used widely across all levels of industry. It is, however, not as readily available as you might expect, and one has to search for sources of the more unusual varieties.

Rubber is not something you can use for a printed project as you would paper. Rubber is highly flexible, so it is very difficult to print on as the ink needs to be as flexible as the substrate itself. The supply of flexible inks is very limited and the choice of colours remains highly restrictive (white being the most common). It is also not possible to deboss the material, as it is too dense. There are, however, flexible PVCs available as alternatives, and they even smell like rubber.

A good source of coloured rubber is domestic floor tiles. These tend to be more rigid than black flooring rubber (as found in factories), but the reverse of the tile can be uneven and rough to allow flooring glue to be applied. It must be stressed that the colours available are all subdued, as they are affected by rubber's natural base-colour. Rubber can be guillotined and die cut, but, given its thickness and slight flexibility, it can be difficult when it comes to finishing. It is advisable to carry out tests to give an indication of likely results.

Latex is a very thin alternative to rubber. Commonly used in fetish clothing, latex can be glued or bonded together to form pouches or covers, for instance. However, latex is very fragile and has a tendency to dry out and fall apart. In addition, rubber bands are a good binding alternative if you do not want to use staples. They come in a wide variety of colours and gauges.

See THREEasFOUR identity — Stiletto nyc [pp.128–130]

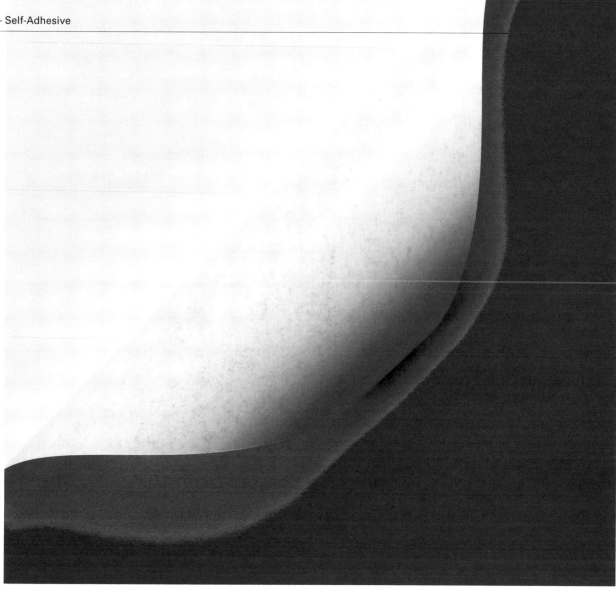

SELF-ADHESIVE

Self-adhesive materials began as gummed papers that needed water applied to the glue to make them adhere. They were taken further in the 1930s by R. Stanton Avery, who developed a self-adhesive sheet that was more pliable and could be applied around curved shapes such as bottles. Another advantage was that this sheet could be repositioned without leaving a sticky residue.

Self-adhesive materials are made with a water-based adhesive, which is roller coated on a silicone-coated backing or release paper. The adhesive is allowed to dry off and the nominated top sheet applied. The adhesive then transfers itself to the top sheet.

Self-adhesive materials are supplied with either a solid or split/crack release paper. Solid-back means you have to peel the release paper back from the edge of the sticker. Crack-back allows you to split the backing paper and get to the adhesive side more quickly. Crack-back may be easier to use but it does have a tendency to show through on the printed side. Also, it prohibits printing on the reverse of the release paper.

At the risk of stating the obvious, self-adhesive materials have a very specific application and they are rarely used outside their role as a label. The range of adhesives available is very wide, from industrial to domestic, so it is advisable to state precisely what the application will be to avoid paying too much for a particular adhesive, the precise function of which may not be necessary.

Self-adhesive materials are available in a number of finishes and colours. However, it is quite common to find a manufacturer's logo repeat-printed on the reverse of the backing paper. This can detract from what you want to print, so if required be careful to specify a plain back. The manufacturing process also means that you can source thicker materials and, in some cases, thicker backing papers, which can give added substance to the printed item. All self-adhesive products can be printed and finished by any process, and they do not pose any problems. The only difficulty to watch out for is that the bigger the self-adhesive panel, the more difficult it will be to apply.

SYNTHETIC PAPER

Synthetic paper is the collective term for a group of substrates developed by a number of companies as alternatives to conventional wood-based paper. They are predominantly characterized by their strength and printability, and have been specifically developed and marketed as waterproof, chemical resistant and tear resistant. Therefore they are stronger than paper, and often easier and more versatile to use. When they are observed at close quarters, some synthetic papers will have a faint iridescent sheen, and most will also have an interesting texture.

Brands of synthetic paper include Polyart, Synplas Synteape, Teslin and Yupo, and there is also a number of polyester films that can be considered as being part of the same family. Despite being regarded as representing a new direction in substrates, synthetic papers all suffer from a myriad of lithographic printing problems (in particular the ink not drying and the material curling), thus they require very specific handling. For example, the majority of printers tend to overcome the issue of ink not drying by applying layer upon layer of varnish after printing, which causes an uneven or orange-peel effect on the print.

Putting aside the caution that needs to be exercised when printing lithographically, these materials do respond well to silk-screen printing and to foil blocking, though embossing results are mixed as the emboss does not stay in the material. They can be perfect bound, though static build-up between the sheets can cause problems. A great advantage of synthetic papers is that, unlike PVC, which cracks when folded, these substrates can be creased and folded without ever snapping.

Not many designers are familiar with the potential of synthetic papers, and merchants shy away from offering them as they appear to sit in so many categories but they do not provide the complete range of conventional applications. With growth in use, synthetic papers will increasingly be seen to be attractive and aesthetically pleasing, which is not always evident from reading the manufacturers' literature.

See Sketch look book — Ich & Kar [pp.155–157]

TYVEK

Tyvek is a registered trademark of the Dupont Company, and is one of those materials that you either love or hate. It is a synthetic material made of high-density polyethylene fibres. These make Tyvek lightweight yet strong, resistant to moisture and tear resistant.

Tyvek was discovered by Dupont employee Jim White, who in 1955 saw white polyethylene fluff coming out of a pipe in an experimental lab. A programme to develop the new material was set up; a year later Dupont submitted a patent application. The proprietary flash-spinning technology, which was the basis for what was to become Tyvek, took several more years to perfect. In 1959, a pilot facility was established for trial applications, such as book covers, tags, labels and certain garments. In 1965, this new engineered sheet structure was registered under the trademark Tyvek, but it was only in April 1967 that commercial production started.

Tyvek is formed by a fully integrated process that uses continuous and very fine fibres of 100 per cent high-density polyethylene, which are randomly distributed and non-directional. The fibres are first flash spun, then are laid as a web on a moving bed, before being bonded together by heat and pressure.

Tyvek superficially resembles paper; for example, it can be written and printed on. It was the medium that New Zealand's driver's licences were printed on from 1986 to 1999, and some countries have printed their currency on it. However, Tyvek cannot be recycled in normal recycling facilities.

It is possible to print Tyvek conventionally, but very few places are set up to print it lithographically. It also has a tendency to curl if the wrong inks are used when screen printed. Whilst it can be foil blocked, the heat of the process can cause the material to cockle.

Rigid versions are available from many leading merchants, but it is the versions used for clothing, or more industrial applications, that may provide more interest to the designer. Their finish appears to be different and the coatings more unusual. Tyvek can, for instance, be utilized as part of the roof of a house. The grey variant resembles matting and strongly displays the spun effect that marks this material out. At present, Tyvek's application is limited by its appearance, and it seems to be consigned to jobs that have either a future or industrial aesthetic. However, Tyvek is a material that should be retained in any studio, as there is always the possibility that it will find its way into a project.

See Visvim product packaging — CUBISM inc.
[pp.182–184]

VELCRO

Velcro-brand fasteners, or hook-and-loop fasteners, consist of two mating components: hook and loop, or 'soft' loop and 'rough' hook. The woven hook tape consists of minute flexible 'hooks', which engage with a mating loop tape comprised of soft 'loops'. When pressed together, the resulting closure is adjustable and highly secure. To reopen, the closure is simply peeled apart.

It was discovered in 1948 by Swiss engineer George de Mestral, who noticed how difficult it was to detach thistles from his clothing while out hunting. The thistle, when viewed under a microscope, revealed a covering of hooks that created this strong adherence. From this, the concept of 'hook and loop' was born. Derived from the first syllables of the French words *velours* (loop) and *crochet* (hook), the Velcro brand name was introduced in 1959 and is used by the Velcro companies to market a wide range of hook-and-loop fasteners.

Velcro has a myriad of applications across a broad spread of industries. To the designer it is an alternative closure device, being readily available in strip and dot form. It is also available in a wide variety of colours from pastels to brights. Caution is needed as some adhesive backings may react with the surface they are applied to, for instance when mounting to flexible PVCs. However, this can be overcome, as a high-frequency weldable version is widely available. The reverse of Velcro-brand or hook-and-loop products, though rough in texture, can be screen printed with bold text.

There are also Velcro straps available that could be applied as a form of binding. A further development from the Velcro companies has been the Velcro-brand paper, where a microscopic hook has been laminated to the reverse of a cast-coated paper, which can be printed digitally, lithographically or by silk screen.

WOOD

The bulk of what we read, buy and consume has its source in paper and board. Both have their roots in wood as the source of their raw material, and wood is in common use by furniture and product designers—it is part of the very essence of what they create.

For the graphic designer there would appear to be little opportunity to employ the material. Indeed, there would not seem to be any reason why you should even consider it. But, if the opportunity does arise, for instance if your client happens to be a timber yard or furniture maker, you do need to be armed with all the necessary information to enable this substrate to be approached with confidence.

In the majority of cases where wood is used, it needs to be thin, have a grain and be capable of being printed on. Designers are often keen to specify a certain type of wood, normally based on a piece of furniture they have spotted, or the flooring in their studio. More often than not, the wood they ask for is either too brittle to be supplied at any less than 20mm thick, or it is too expensive. A type of wood that is suitable, however, is tulipwood, which can be stained and varnished to look like any wood, and also has a very good grain to it.

Silk-screen printing is a tried and tested method of applying a logo to the surface of wood. If the wood is hard enough then it should be possible to foil block it. Some wood workshops have etching tools that allow an engraved, almost branded, effect. This process is costly and time-consuming, and a brown screen print has much the same effect, and without the disadvantage of the burnt wood smell.

Sourcing wood is not simply a matter of visiting the local timber yard. You will find that shop-fitting companies are a useful source of supply as they understand issues around getting the right finish and the sizes you might require as a graphic designer.

See *The North Face: Unlimited* — Saturday [pp.161–163]

PROCESS

INTRODUCTION

Processes can be divided into a number of relevant areas. Variants of the lithographic printing process are the most commonly encountered, and, where ink to material is concerned, each process has very specific characteristics that are peculiar only to itself. The processes featured here have been included because they offer an alternative or, as in the case of screen printing, provide a number of exciting opportunities to print on a wider range of materials. There are great possibilities for both experimentation and adaptation.

A number of the processes listed are a component part of the production of a printed project. This can range from die cutting to binding and, possibly, to the various types of closure that can be utilized.

Finally, a number of alternative processes usually relevant for packaging have been included, with suggestions for other applications. These processes may offer routes to some level of creativity that may not have been explored before.

Exploiting the possibilities of each of these processes is reliant on an understanding of key areas. These areas are research, cost and lead time. They are crucial because, without an understanding of these, no project can develop efficiently and also benefit from the use of something that has not been tried before.

Research begins with identifying a process that appeals aesthetically, and may have an application to the execution of your design. You may come across an everyday item or a piece of packaging whose source needs to be found. In the case of previously printed items it may be a case of contacting the producer or designer to ascertain what this process is. Sometimes this line of enquiry may yield the identity of the manufacturer. However, this information may well prove to be a jealously guarded secret.

It becomes more difficult when the item reveals nothing that would characterize its provenance. Look for suppliers producing specific items for specific applications. There may be something that can be adapted to your needs. Hopefully the pages that follow will provide images and words that allow you to appraise processes more efficiently.

The more industrial a process, the greater the cost of producing mouldings or tools prior to manufacture. Printing processes will also have set-up costs, but their price rarely has this impact on final value. In the case of such processes as thermoforming or injection moulding, the tooling could be viewed as expensive, but this should not put you off exploring various sources of supply. Your production quantity may be low enough to warrant the use of a more rudimentary tool, or your supplier may offer suggestions as to how a design could be modified to achieve a better price. Careful questioning may also reveal competitive suppliers within the same field.

Lead time can vary from process to process. The more reliant on tooling, the longer it will take to prototype, develop and produce a product. You have to be conscious of this factor. A long production and delivery schedule may preclude the use of a particular process for your project.

Unlike materials, the use of a process needs to be demonstrated if someone needs to be convinced to sanction its use. Building a healthy dialogue with a supplier will yield examples that show its application or allow you to prototype your ideas at little or no cost. It is all about engaging and enthusing everyone involved in the project to allow new ideas to develop.

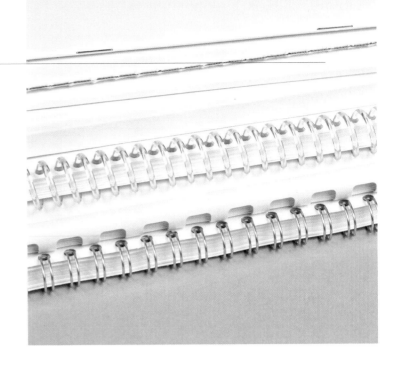

BINDING

Binding is one of the elements of the finishing process of any printed book or pamphlet. There are many binding methods, some of which are automated and some of which can only be completed by hand.

Saddle Stitching — Saddle or wire stitching is the most common, and one of the cheapest, binding techniques. Printed sheets are bound by passing one or more metal wires, or staples, through the pages and covers. The two most frequent methods of saddle stitching are spine stitching or flat stitching. With spine stitching the staples are driven through the folds on folded sheets, whereas with flat stitching they go through the outer edge of flat sheets.

It is almost impossible to get coloured staples as the pressure of stitching powder-coated wire will cause the colour coating to crack. It is possible to colour the wires, after stitching, with a solvent-based marker pen. The results, however, can be mixed.

Singer Sewing — Singer sewing, as the name implies, requires the use of a sewing machine to create a stitched line. As with saddle stitching, you can sew along the spine or on the outer edge of flat sheets. There is a maximum number of sheets possible for Singer sewing, which may prohibit your use of this method for bulky documents. Singer sewing tends not to be as uniform as other methods of binding, with loose threads left at the head and foot of the spine, which can create a more hand-finished effect.

Perfect Binding — Perfect binding, or adhesive binding, is a common binding method when there is a great number of pages to be bound together. All magazines and paperback books are bound in this way.

The binding process involves first collating together the inside pages of the item, then notching or shaving off a small portion of the pages on this bound edge. A flexible adhesive is applied and the cover is attached. Note that certain papers are more receptive to the glues used for perfect binding than others. Uncoated paper is particularly receptive while coated paper is not able to absorb the glue so easily, which can cause the adhesive to split over time.

Thread Binding — Thread binding is one of the oldest and strongest of all forms of binding. It is principally employed in the binding of hardbound books. It involves putting the printed and section-folded sheets into the correct order and trimming them. Instead of stapling or gluing them together, they are thread stitched together on the spine. The cover is then glued on. One trend in recent years has been to expose this binding, and also vary the thread colour to make a feature of it. In addition, the trimming of the ragged edges of the page has been omitted to create the feeling of a deconstructed book.

Wire Binding — There are three variables to this form of binding: wiro binding, spiral binding and comb binding. Common to all these methods are the trimming down of single sheets, collation with a cover and then binding. The sheets will require cutting on the relevant machine prior to the wire or plastic comb being attached. A more industrial machine will be able to cut through thicker cover materials.

The disadvantage of spiral binding is that the pages never align, head to foot, when turned. This is because the stock is turning on the spiral of the wire. However, any wire binding is a cheap and efficient way of binding documents, and allows the use of varying materials within the text.

The look of wire binding has been augmented by the introduction of all manner of wire and comb colours and finishes. Not all of the colours are commonly available and you may have to purchase more of this binding material than your project requires.

CARTON MAKING

Carton making is seen as the cheaper alternative to rigid box making, but it serves a wider variety of needs. For consumer packaging, where price is an issue, it is certainly the preferred option. However, its aesthetic value can be augmented by the use of substrates beyond conventional printed folding boxboard. In addition, from a logistics point of view, cartons are better than rigid boxes as they can be packed flat and transported with greater ease.

Cartons tend to rely on flaps, along with a single gluing, to enable them to close, as the majority of these packaging forms are created for automatic manufacture. Cartons made for everyday consumption are full of tiny hidden details that can be exploited if you look closely. Try examining the way that the tabs and flaps on pill cartons have been cut away and nicked to ensure that the carton locks in place when closed. Pull a carton apart and look at all the registration markings where it has been glued shut.

Cartons are used across a variety of industries and products, with certain forms being indigenous to certain applications. The idiosyncrasies of these cartons could be cross-pollinated into other areas: pharmaceutical packaging could be employed as packaging for perfume, for example.

The production of a carton involves its design and prototyping, the creation of a cutting forme, die cutting and gluing. Most prototyping is now undertaken by CAD cutting machinery, where basic coordinates are plotted to produce not only a physical carton but also a digital cutter trace, enabling the designer to plan the artwork. While the CAD result is very finessed, a cardboard engineer, if you are lucky enough to find one, can provide an analogue experience as well as a memory of ideas that a machine cannot replicate. For example, there may have been types of closures, in vogue decades ago and remembered by the engineer, that you can apply to your designs.

The inclusion of a cutting-forme maker or a die cutter in the project is also important. They can advise on problems in cutting and creasing a carton, and whether the idea is economical to produce. For instance, you need to know how to maximize the number of cartons cut from one sheet without wasting too much material.

Cartons need not be produced from paper and board; it is worthwhile exploring the shapes and forms and how they could be applied to synthetic materials such as rigid PVCs and polypropylenes.

See *Ladies and Gentlemen We are Floating in Space*, Spiritualized — Farrow Design/Spaceman [pp.200–202]

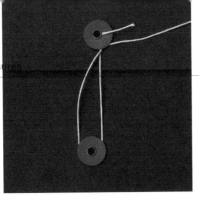

CLOSURES

Closures—which, in the context of this book, means the various methods in which a box or book can be kept shut—are a matter of taste and are dependent on the intentions of the project. Undertaken as one part of the finishing process, they can be an obtrusive component of the exterior of the work, insomuch as they will be the first thing the user interacts with.

Disc and String — This type of closure originated with the legal profession. It is used principally on envelopes and folders housing documents that need to be securely fastened and accessed quickly. It consists of discs riveted onto the opening parts. The machinery that is needed to achieve this is quite specialized, as both discs have to be riveted. One disc has a length of string attached to it that ties around the other disc in a figure-of-eight configuration.

The discs themselves tend to be made from a pressed cardboard and the string from cotton. It is possible to have these discs made from the same material as the item you are producing; however, they will not then be as strong as pressed cardboard and can buckle when tied with the string.

Magnets — These have become a popular method of closure in recent years, mainly thanks to the satisfactory click as the two poles align and snap shut. The most common form is a magnetic strip, which can be supplied in varying widths. Some individuals are put off by this strip, as it can be quite thick and conspicuous when shut. There are also magnetic discs available, but they are problematic because of their bulk.

Another aspect of magnets that may worry clients is their brownish-black colour, but it is not possible to get different coloured magnets. Clients and designers alike are often under the mistaken apprehension that if a magnet is obscured under a piece of card or lining then this overcomes the issue. In fact, it only obliterates the magnetism. A better suggestion is to make a feature of it. Make the magnet bigger or silk-screen a logo over it.

It is a good idea to ask the supplier to provide the strip cut to length, to ensure that the poles meet. It is also a good idea to check that the adhesive backing of the magnet sticks to your particular substrate.

Velcro — Velcro needs to be assessed as a closure in a similar way to magnets. One of the key tests is to ensure that the adhesive sticks to your chosen substrate. There is a good selection of colours that can be used to match or contrast; Velcro can also be supplied as a strip or as dots in a range of sizes. However, as the Velcro system creates a very strong contact, you can find that some dots may tear off the substrate when opened.

Press Studs — Press studs tend to be best employed with more rigid materials such as polypropylene. They are attached by riveting to the substrate. It can sometimes be difficult to find a press stud closure that matches the overall aesthetic of the project. Commonly available colours tend to be bright primaries, black, white, gold and bright chrome.

Elastic — When attached to the back cover of a book or the lining of a box, elastic presents the user with an interesting closure alternative. You are not directly shutting and pressing the object closed. You are merely holding it together in a similar way to putting an elastic band around documents. Elastic can be sourced from haberdashers or ribbon suppliers, with the widths and colours available varying from country to country.

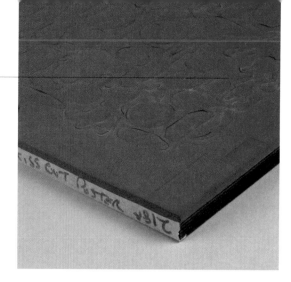

DIE CUTTING

Die cutting is a common process used to cut a range of sheet materials, including paper, cardboard, rubber and plastic. Most standard cardboard boxes or packages are made using this relatively straightforward technique. In addition to cutting out shapes, this method of cutting can be used to create creases, perforations and slits.

The die is produced by a die or cutting-forme maker out of a flat base or substrate that is usually made out of high-density plywood. The die maker uses a band saw or laser cutter to cut precisely positioned slits into the wood. The die maker then cuts and bends a steel rule, essentially an elongated razor blade made out of hardened steel, and positions it into the slits in the substrate to form the cutting edge. Finally, rubber pads, known as ejection rubber, are adhered to the substrate to help eject the material after it has been cut. The wood, steel rule and ejection rubber combine together to create what is commonly referred to as a cutting forme.

Once the die maker has completed the cutting forme, it is immediately ready for production. The die is attached to the top surface or platen of a die-cutting press, which will provide the force required for the job. The material to be cut is positioned below the die and then the press is put into action. If registration is an issue, the material is positioned against a stop or in a locating nest. The cutting edges of the steel rule penetrate through the material until they come into contact with the bottom platen; then the press reverses and the cut part is exposed. In some applications, a softer material is placed below the material to accept the cutting surfaces of the steel rule.

Perforations and creases are made with a special steel creasing rule that is positioned on the same forme. Creases sometimes require the use of a secondary die, called a matrix, which is positioned on the opposite side of the press and aligned with the creasing rule; when configured properly very crisp creases can be created in the materials. Sometimes heated platens are used when plastic parts are being fabricated to improve the quality of the creases and cuts.

In high-volume die-cutting operations, fully automatic machines will be used. With these machines, the material to be cut is automatically fed into the press and located in the proper position. The steel-rule die is pressed through the material and the pressure is released. The cut piece is removed, along with any scrap material or waste, and then the next piece is positioned to repeat the process.

See *Werk No.13 Jan de Cock* — Work [pp.203–204]

DIE STAMPING

Die stamping is the traditional way of embossing stationery and invitations, using an engraved plate or die. Engraving means 'to carve into', which accurately describes what the engraver does to create a design in relief on the face of a metal die. The completed engraved die is mounted in a die press, which exerts a massive pressure as the die comes into contact with the paper. This pressure ensures the precision and depth of image that are always associated with die stamping.

The inks used in die-stamping have traditionally been oil based and slow drying. But, since the advent of laser printers, water-based inks have been introduced that do not melt at high temperatures, allowing their use for stationery. A die can also be used entirely without ink, in a procedure called blind embossing.

Printing with an engraved die can introduce all manner of effects. In general, because the design depends on relief and the ink is deposited in the areas of the die that have been cut away (those below the surface of metal coming into contact with the paper), the printed design is raised above the paper, i.e. embossed. There is

no such thing as multi-colour die stamping; each colour has to be individually laid down with extreme accuracy. This all makes for a much slower process, and it is more expensive than conventional lithography. However, the thickness of the ink and the wonderful tactile effects more than compensate for this. When metallic colours are employed a burnished effect is even possible. This is achieved by running an ink-free die over ink previously deposited. By applying extra pressure, the ink image on the page is forced into the die, thus creating a superbly embossed, brilliant finish.

Dies are usually made from steel and are hardened after engraving to allow for prolonged use. Copper plates are often best for shorter runs, while brass for blind embossing achieves smoother contours to the design. Die stamping also allows you to print on much thicker paper stocks than normal.

Die stamping is rarely considered or used by most designers, but like thermography it offers an alternative to more conventional print processes, creating a tactile and luxurious finish.

DIP MOULDING

Dip moulding is employed across a wide variety of industries and applications. You only have to look at the handle grips on garden tools and prams or the coverings on electrical cables to understand its use. In effect it provides a sleeve of PVC to protect or cushion, but there is no reason why its application could not be extended into the packaging of numerous other products, from CDs to perfume.

Compared to injection moulding, dip moulding lends itself to low-volume production runs and the development of projects. It is also versatile enough to cater for volume production when needed. In addition, it has far cheaper tooling costs for both prototypes and production tooling. If the shape is straightforward then it can be turned on a lathe or milling machine. The preferred material for tooling is aluminium, with more complex shapes being made first from a wooden pattern then cast in aluminium.

The tooling, or 'male former', is heated and immersed in a tank of cold liquid PVC. The longer it remains in this tank, the thicker the wall of the moulding. It is then taken out and is placed in a curing oven, followed by further immersion in cold water for cooling. After this cooling, the moulded item is finally removed from the tooling using compressed air.

The material can be supplied in a wide range of softnesses, measured by what is known as its 'Shore hardness' (the lower the Shore hardness number, the softer the material). If you wish to maximize the strength of the moulding, grooves can be machined into the tool. This will result in internal ribbing inside a moulding, which provides a greater degree of rigidity.

The PVC material can be supplied in a wide range of standard colours, and Pantone matching is available. However, because of its common applications, samples tend to be red, blue or black. The finish of the material can also be varied, depending on your requirements. This can vary across matt, gloss and textured finishes. After moulding, very little finishing work needs to be done to the moulded shape.

The dip-moulding process does not lend itself to forming text out of the tooling since it would be difficult to strip the mould off without damaging the finished product. The surface can be printed, with silk-screen printing giving the greatest flexibility. Pad printing, which allows printing on uneven, three-dimensional surfaces, can be employed for more complicated shapes.

This process does offer a very specific finish and feel. Given its synthetic and tactile nature, it lends itself well to some of the packaging applications listed earlier (such as CDs and perfumes), although good samples will be essential in the presentation of an idea to clients, and will help generate other thoughts on how any given project can be developed.

FLEXOGRAPHY

Flexography, or flexo, is a method of printing that is most commonly used for packaging, plastic bags and corrugated boxes. It is most effective on uncoated packaging materials such as corrugated cardboard.

Flexo is so named because it was first developed as a method of printing onto corrugated cardboard, which has an extremely uneven surface. The printing-plate surface must always maintain contact with the cardboard, which it does by being flexible. Also, unprinted high points on the cardboard must not get printed by ink remnants that are not on the plate surface, and this is achieved by ensuring that there is a sufficient depth for the non-print areas of the plate.

A flexo print is achieved by creating a mirrored master of the required image as a three-dimensional relief in a rubber or polymer material. A measured amount of ink is deposited upon the surface of the printing plate or cylinder. The print surface then rotates, contacting with the print material and transferring the ink.

The applications of flexography may be somewhat limited. Its main advantage is that it is cheaper to print on corrugated packaging using this method than screen printing. It is best used as a printing method for typography. The origination and printing method does not lend itself readily to the printing of half-tones.

One printing disadvantage is that the inks used are not as opaque as silk-screen inks. This is because of a deposit of ink onto the surface of the material from the rubber printing plate. A lot of people are put off by the resulting ink shadowing around areas of text. In fact, this lack of sharpness could be turned into an advantage if you are looking for a utilitarian aesthetic.

See Damien Hirst print transit box [pp.092–094]

FOIL BLOCKING

The process of foil blocking evolved from the technique of gold-leaf embellishment, in which a very thin film of beaten gold leaf was applied to a surface; this would be decorated, through pressure, with a series of tools, to achieve the required pattern. The resulting print would then be cleaned of any excess gold, which was returned to the gold beater for reprocessing into more leaf. This was a time-consuming and costly process, and though there are still experts working in real gold leaf today an alternative process needed to be developed. New technology has led to improvements in synthetic foils, including gold colours. These foils can be applied in a thin layer to a material through the use of heat and pressure. Foil blocking operates as an addition to other printing methods, allowing metallic finishes to be applied to a surface.

There is a huge range of foils, including metallic, colour and clear, and some more unusual holographic or decorative foils, which are made up with 'shim lines'. These lines are created when the edge of a foil is butted up against the edge of the same pattern, like wallpaper. Some of the foil suppliers have managed to minimize this phenomenon but you should still watch out for it. Obviously, solid colours do not present this problem.

There are strict rules governing the process of foil blocking, which should not be ignored. For instance, you cannot foil on top of foil; if you apply foil on the reverse, and then foil in register on the front, this will only serve to remove the foil from the side on which you have just printed. If you wish to try to bend rules by attempting over-foiling, for example, you need to be present while the process is being applied.

Foil blocking can be used for stationery and letterheads. A potential problem is that when this stationery is being printed on, the foil can reheat and peel away from the paper, dependent on the type of printer used. If planning to use foil blocking for such purposes, you should test the foil across all office printers to ensure compatibility. Foil blocking is sometimes considered to be a somewhat over-decorative process, and you only have to look at perfume packaging to understand that its perceived value is luxury. However, mixing up substrates with clear foils can produce interesting effects, most notably on synthetic materials such as Tyvek. In addition, foiling in colours that are a close match to the substrate colour is a route worth experimenting with.

See Nike iD dossier — Baby [pp.068–070]

HF WELDING

HF (or high-frequency) welding is also known as RF (radio-frequency) welding or dielectric sealing. The principle behind the process is the use of high-frequency radio energy to produce a molecular agitation in the materials being processed to such a degree that they melt and weld together, typically forming a bond that is as strong as the original material.

To achieve the weld, flexible material, commonly flexible PVC, is placed between a machined brass die (with areas representing the desired weld pattern) and a platen on an RF machine. The head of the machine comes down and generates pressure. The RF comes on, is channelled through the material in the pattern areas only, and fuses the materials together at those points.

RF tooling is usually run 'cold'—once the RF is turned off, the material stops being heated but remains under pressure. This means that it is possible to heat, weld and cool the material under compression in an instant.

The welding tool can be engraved, which gives the entire welded area a decorative appearance, or you can incorporate lettering to emboss the welded area. Also, by incorporating a cutting edge adjacent to the welding surface, the process can simultaneously weld and cut a material.

It is possible to integrate seals, similar to those on freezer bags, during the process, allowing a pouch to be made, for example. There are even HF-weldable Velcro products available, which can provide an alternative form of closure. To create rigidity for items such as a folder cover, panels of board can be encapsulated inside the flexible material on welding. If a softer cover is required, then use of a thinner board or polypropylene for the panels can create the desired result. This approach could even be considered as a packaging alternative, although three-dimensional constructions do tend to stretch the capabilities of this process.

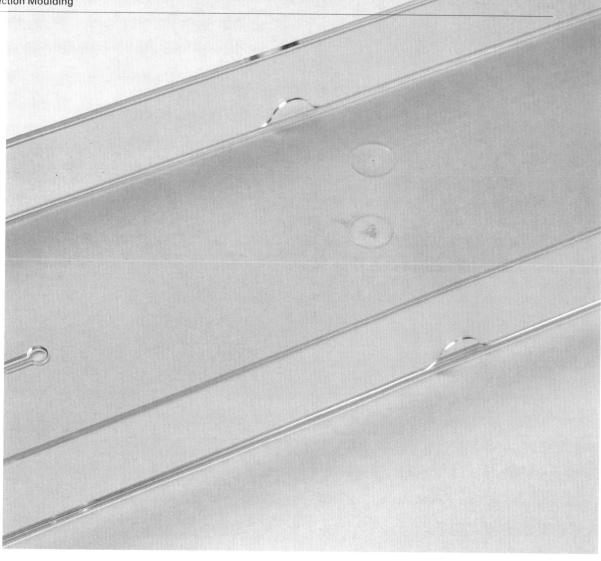

INJECTION MOULDING

Look at a shampoo-bottle top, a CD case and all manner of other items around you. The likelihood is that they have been injection moulded. During the injection-moulding process, polymer granules are fed from a bin or hopper into a heated barrel that houses a rotating screw. These granules, melted by heat and friction, are forced through a valve under pressure. The screw is forced back during this process and is then pushed forward by a hydraulic ram. This action injects material into the mould cavity. The tool is held closed under pressure until the plastic cools and sets hard into the shape inside the tool. The screw starts to move back for the next moulding. The tool then opens and the finished plastic part is ejected or removed. The tool is closed and the whole process starts again.

This process relies on complicated tooling, which is a great deal more expensive than equivalent tooling for other processes, such as thermoforming. The pressures brought to bear with this type of moulding require a tool that has to be cast and engineered with extreme accuracy. There has to be a high level of liaison with the manufacturer to achieve the best results. Collaboration is very important at all stages of the process.

On the surfaces of injection mouldings, you will notice, on occasion, a circular depression. This is the point at which the material has been injected into and flows around the tool. In certain instances—dependent on the design of the moulding—this can interfere with the aesthetics of the product. Dialogue with the mould maker is critical to ensure that this does not compromise an idea, or to see if it can be integrated into the design.

Injection moulding offers exciting opportunities to create highly finessed packaging solutions. As a process it can be sourced and utilized nationally and internationally. The manufacturing method and materials employed are clearly understood wherever it is produced. It is unfortunate that its tooling costs can be high compared with other processes. However, the results can outstrip the expense, and it can be worth convincing the client, and others, to employ it.

See *The Brick* — Hugh Brown [pp.137–139]

INKS

There is a limited selection of ink systems that can be applied to materials beyond conventional Pantone or process colours. In most cases these systems work best when applied via silk-screen printing, although some can be printed lithographically. Below are some inks that deserve special mention.

Scented Ink — Scented inks can be supplied in a wide selection of smells and can also be synthesized to use a specific fragrance. They tend to be suspended, at a molecular level, within a semi-clear base. This is then screen printed onto the required substrate. However, it is important to be aware that because the scented inks are water based they can only be printed on paper or board that has not been sealed. On other substrates, water-based ink does not adhere and will scratch off.

The scent has a tendency to lose its potency over time. If you plan on using a specific existing fragrance, this will require a very close liaison with the ink maker. Perfume clients will often be reluctant to supply the base fragrance as the blend is bound up in secrecy.

Heat-Sensitive Ink — Heat-sensitive inks can be supplied in a limited range of colours. However, clients tend to prefer black as it produces the most dramatic results. The heat-sensitive component is suspended in a semi-clear base and works best when screen printed. The reactive temperature can be varied according to climatic conditions. As with scented inks, the system is water based and, consequently, it is supplied for printing on paper-based substrates. It can work on plastic, but a number of layers of varnish will need to be applied for it to key in. This is time-consuming and is not very cost-effective. Heat-sensitive ink also has a tendency to scuff if not properly sealed. It can look best when laminated, particularly with black, as this intensifies the colour.

Rub-Removable Ink — Normally the preserve of lottery scratch cards or other promotional items, rub-removable ink is latex based. It is supplied as a metallic, as its function is to obliterate what it overprints. The ink is quite fragile and difficult to work with, but it can be effective when printed in solid areas, giving a rubberized feel and communicating effectively the message that the printed area needs to be handled with care.

Pearlescent and Iridescent Inks — These inks can be printed on all substrates and create a different shade of metallic colour dependent on the proximity of the viewer to the printed item. They tend to be used on gift cards but also work well as solid areas with text reversed out.

Other Ink Systems — Other ink systems include light-sensitive ink (which only reacts in natural sunlight), glow-in-the-dark ink and glitter ink. It is strongly recommended that you research all these areas of printing with an eye to what is available outside your own country, not just within it. Inks are easily transportable and persistent research will provide you with something unique.

See *Scratch and Sniff* EP, Future Loop Foundation — Big Active [pp.191–193]

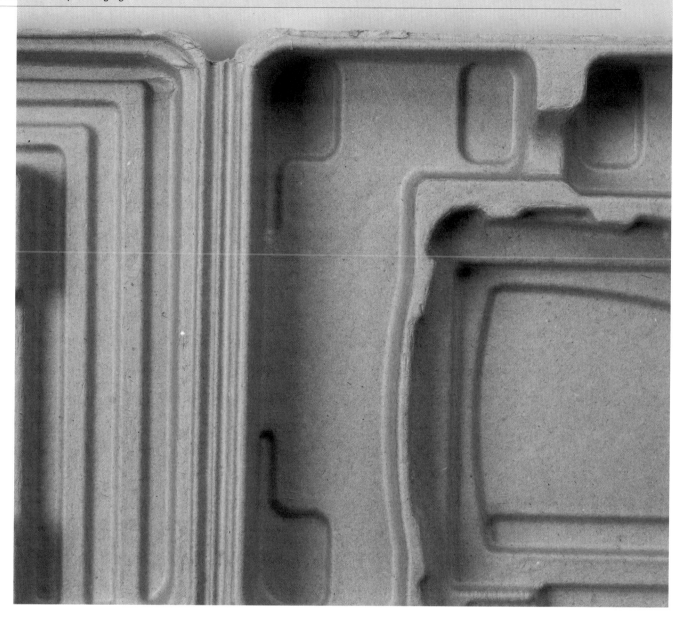

PULP PACKAGING

Pulp packaging is most commonly employed as protective packaging for goods while in transit. You see it used as edge corners around radiators or doors and sinks. As it is usually manufactured from recycled and biodegradable materials, it is increasingly used as a 'green' alternative to plastic, often for items such as food trays or disposable medical containers.

The product is made from pulp and goes through a similar manufacturing process to that used for grey board. However, as it then has to be turned into shapes, the pulp is formed on a gauze, using slight suction to keep it in place. The thickness of its walls is of optimum importance: too thin and they will not be self-supporting; too thick and the build-up of the pulp will stop the suction. Properly designed, pulp will perform better as packaging than expanded polystyrene and other plastic-based cushioning.

Tooling can prove to be inexpensive—it goes through similar stages as thermoforming tooling. Logos can be integrated into this tooling as either raised or depressed areas. Production runs may have to be quite large for the process to be cost-effective, but this may depend on other packaging being manufactured at the time, and also whether your run can tie in with the schedules and quantities of compatible products.

Pulp packaging can be dyed to a colour, but this can prove to be very costly as the machinery will need a thorough cleaning afterwards, as the entire production system will have become contaminated. Coloured paper or white pulp can be used as an alternative.

Previously understood as cost-prohibitive, pulp bears further investigation as an interesting packaging solution, offering a more environmentally sympathetic alternative to plastic-based moulding applications.

RIGID BOX MAKING

Rigid boxes are among the more luxurious and desirable forms of packaging. They are often handmade, so a certain aura surrounds them, and the nature of their construction means that the boxes feel substantial and permanent. For this reason, any luxury product, from cut-crystal glasses to handmade shoes, will utilize this type of construction, as the boxes serve to add a layer of importance to their contents. Versions of this type of packaging can be made by machine, but the choice of material and construction is much more limited.

Put simply, a rigid box consists of a hard base material, such as grey board, which is cut to shape, fixed together to form a box, then covered in cloth, paper or vinyl. The box can be lined, usually using a coloured, uncoated paper. A common construction is a lift-off lid, which can be difficult to remove, particularly on a larger box, because of the vacuum created when the box is shut. Thumb cuts, die cut on either side of the lid after it has been covered, can help, but will be a little unsightly, as they cut through the covering material to reveal the substrate used for the base box. A compromise is to vary the depth of your lid—on a hinged-lid rigid box it may be possible to make the closure in a chevron shape, for example. However, because the box is covered, you can end up with a bulk of covering material where it has overlapped in creating the closure.

Larger boxes are more difficult to cover and are therefore more expensive, because their construction is more labour-intensive. Covering material needs to be cut to shape then glued on the reverse prior to application. At this stage the covering material usually has a tendency to curl, and the larger the box the more staff are required to deal with the problem. In addition, producing short-run boxes utilizing a printed paper can pose problems in ensuring the accurate alignment of the print along all sides.

Lining the box is a further added cost, although it does tidy up the edges of the covering material when it returns into the lid and base. The base material can be supplied ready lined in either white or black, which can be helpful if cost is a problem. Because of the method of construction, it is very difficult to make a rigid box any shallower than 15 to 25mm. In such cases it may be wiser to consider using a cardboard carton.

Producing a rigid box is an extremely satisfying experience. Prototypes appear almost as the finished work, and throughout you get the sense that you are part of a process that belongs to a tradition that has existed before the onset of machines, and is more of a dialogue with craft.

See Makri jewellery packaging — Spin [pp.077–079]

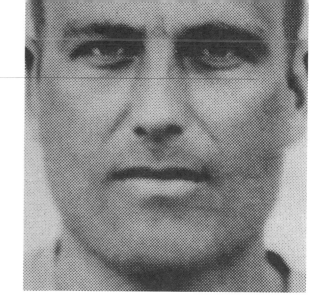

SCREEN PRINTING

The process of screen printing (often called silk-screen printing) offers possibly the greatest versatility for the designer. It is flexible insomuch as it affords the opportunity to experiment with many different materials and ink systems. Screen printing can be automated, but can also be produced on a hand bench.

A screen is made of a piece of porous and finely woven fabric (originally silk, but typically polyester or nylon since the 1940s), stretched over a rectangular wood or aluminium frame. Areas of the screen are blocked off with a non-permeable material—a stencil—which is a negative of the image to be printed.

The screen is placed on top of the substrate to be printed. Ink is placed on top of the screen, and a squeegee, or rubber blade, is used to push the ink evenly into the screen openings and onto the substrate. Ink passes through the open spaces in the screen onto the material below; then the screen is lifted away. The screen can be reused after cleaning. If more than one colour is being printed on the same surface, the ink is allowed to dry and then the process is repeated with another screen and a different colour of ink.

Stencils were originally cut from paper or were painted directly onto the screen using a filler material impermeable to ink. Today, the method in most common use is the photo-emulsion technique. The original image is placed on a transparent film as a positive. This overlay is placed over the emulsion-coated screen and then exposed to a strong light. The areas that are not opaque in the overlay allow light to reach the emulsion, which hardens and sticks to the screen. The screen is washed off thoroughly. Those areas of emulsion that were not exposed to light, corresponding to the image on the overlay, dissolve and wash away, leaving a negative stencil of the image attached to the screen.

The process of screen printing is charged with an immediacy that can't be compared with other processes. Screen shops smell like no other factories. The choice of material is without limit, and the opportunities for experimentation equally so. If a material is sourced and there is time to experiment, then a screen shop is the first place to visit to try things out.

See *365: AIGA Year in Design 24* — COMA [pp.089–091]

THERMOFORMING

Thermoforming is a method of processing sheets of plastic-based substrates. The material is heated to its particular thermoforming temperature and immediately shaped. At this temperature the material is very supple, allowing it to be formed very quickly to the desired shape with the minimum amount of force. This pressure is maintained until the part has cooled, when it is trimmed out of the sheet used to hold it during production.

As long ago as the Roman period, imported tortoise shell had been formed, using hot oil, into cooking utensils. But thermoforming developed rapidly during the Second World War, when increased production of plastics made it the perfect process for manufacturing aircraft canopies and gun turrets, giving maximum visibility with minimum distortion. As with many processes and materials, this adoption for military uses helped to legitimize thermoforming in the eyes of the commercial sector and, in addition, it had become a tried and tested technology, well resourced with skilled experts and with plant equipment.

For high production runs it is necessary to invest in tooling that will withstand the rigours of the process outlined above, although this tooling remains cheaper than that associated with injection moulding. Thermoforming tooling is generally machined or cast aluminium, but for shorter runs tooling can be made from wood, plaster, resin or other materials, although such tooling will degrade very quickly.

Because thermoforming is used for more industrial applications it is often not considered suitable for more aesthetic purposes—people encounter thermoformed plastic as packaging for items such as screwdrivers or chocolate. Consequently it is usually viewed as a clear form of presentation packaging, dressed up with printed cardboard to obscure it. Given the wealth of materials available, and the different reactions that they undergo during forming, this is an area ripe for exploration. An interesting example is the use of thermoformed high-density foams in sportswear protection and shoes.

Clearly, thermoforming is a very precise process. The material has to be consistent and the sheet must be heated evenly to the correct processing temperature. For instance, overheating causes degradation and burning —this can create interesting results as the material warps and bulges. This will produce a random effect across the production run, but it may well be difficult for the manufacturer to maintain. If this is the desired effect, then a thorough consultation needs to be undertaken with the supplier.

The initial costs (prototype tooling, manufacturing tooling and run costs) can make the cost of this process prohibitive. However, thermoforming does introduce alternative possibilities to a project. It is also an ideal introduction to an appreciation of other manufacturing processes beyond conventional printing. It represents a window into understanding the properties of more industrial and mechanized fabrication, creating a primer for understanding budgets, timings and pitfalls. It serves to remove designers from their computers and focus their energies on a very real production method where ideas can take shape instantly.

See The/Le Garage poster — Graphic Thought Facility [pp.149–151]

THERMOGRAPHY

Thermography, or relief printing, is normally the preserve of high-quality stationery products. Its raised effect adds another dimension to the item, in a similar way to foil blocking or die stamping.

Thermographic printing is a multi-stage process. First, the printed sheet of paper or board drops off the printing press onto a conveyor. This conveyor moves the wet ink on the sheet underneath the thermographic powder, which is shaken on top of the entire sheet. The powder attaches to the wet ink. The extra powder is then vacuumed off. Next, the coated sheet passes through an oven at a very high temperature. In order to obtain the best thermographic printing results, off-set lithography equipment is recommended although the process can be completed by using letterpress equipment as well, particularly on thicker boards.

A common misconception is that thermographic powder is coloured. The powder is clear—it is the print underneath that gives the colour. The powder can be tinted to make it pearlescent, or can have glitter added to give a sparkling effect. The introduction of sand makes it feel like sandpaper. Metallics are also available, along with a limited palette of pastel and fluorescent colours. Despite its expensive appearance, the costs of thermography are reasonable, though it does require research, as the number of suppliers of this process is dwindling.

One potential problem with thermography is that thermographic ink can melt if exposed later to similarly high temperatures, from laser printers in particular. Another problem is that an uneven finish may be left on the ink. However, powders are currently being developed to harden and cure in such a way as to create a smoother finish to the thermographed area.

See Marc Atlan Design, Inc. business card —
Marc Atlan Design, Inc. [pp.083–085]

PRINT

INTRODUCTION

All the case studies featured here share a common characteristic of engagement and immersion in the manufacturing process. This section is not to be regarded as a compendium of the most esoteric or experimental works, but each example has endeavoured to push a project in a new direction while discovering something unique to itself along the way.

Each case study is captioned with its title and the name of the designer. Also included are the principal materials and processes used in the project. These can be cross-referenced in the index, allowing you to look up further details in the earlier materials and process sections. You will notice that not all of these materials and processes have been featured in the case studies. This is intentional as the gaps serve as a springboard for the reader to be among the first to apply them.

I have tried to steer clear of explaining too much about who the designers are—some details have been left in to give the case study context, and they may on occasion reveal that some designers are not commonly regarded as protagonists or leading participants in the field of print or packaging production. Companies such as M/M (Paris) or designers such as Peter Saville are known for their art direction and management of the creative development of their clients' work. They may not, however, be commonly recognized for their interest in and passion for print production, or for their use of materials and techniques. Hopefully these examples will go some way to redressing such misconceptions.

I have avoided showing much work that has been produced for promotional purposes, as this usually means limited quantities and limitless budgets. Most of the products in the case studies are commercially available, or have been in the past. Also, the selection is not about presenting the designers' most current work or even the work they favour as their best. The criterion for selection, as stated before, is that each project shares the common characteristic of a preoccupation with manufacturing and with technique.

I have also endeavoured to tease out the reasons why certain selections were made. In certain instances the designer had no complicated reason as to why a substrate was employed. Helena Ichbiah, for example, had no compunction in using synthetic papers, whereas, from experience, a number of designers are ignorant of such materials or are even scared of using them. It may be second nature to some to employ screen printing, but instil fear in others. Hopefully my selection will empower the reader to consider processes and materials other than those which might seem obvious.

In the majority of the case studies, no other executions, materials, processes or finishing methods were considered. This emphasizes the designers' strength of resolve in pursuing their idea to its conclusion and also shows that all possible research was undertaken to find the best solution. Although all print work encounters problems, a healthy relationship with your suppliers can assist in resolving difficulties, so minor irritations need not turn into a disaster.

The response to the case studies shown here has always been positive, with some of the work winning major awards. Criticism is always from the designers themselves, wishing that they'd had more time and a bigger budget.

removed for

urposes

Materials
Acrylic, Paper (Boxboard; Lining)

Processes
Carton Making, Etching

NOTING ABSENCE
ANNA BLESSMANN AND PETER SAVILLE

Noting Absence is a collaboration between the artist Anna Blessmann and Peter Saville. Created as a saleable art piece, the project consists of acrylic signs housed in cardboard archive boxes. Each piece is an interpretation of the notices utilized by museums and art galleries to mark the space left by a piece of work temporarily removed for cleaning or loaned to another establishment. While these signs usually denote the absence of an object, in this case the signs themselves became the object.

Quite often this type of sign is hastily produced on a piece of paper or cardboard. Saville and Blessmann, however, wanted to create something more permanent, but which retained a connection to the museum environment. The pair achieved this by creating the artworks from acrylic—a material that would be commonly found to create signage in an institutional setting.

The typography on the signs was created by etching and then infilling with ink, creating a tougher finish than screen printing and imbuing the finished piece with a greater sense of permanence and value. In the course of this process the surface of the acrylic is engraved and then paint is spread across the whole sheet. The excess is wiped away, leaving paint in indented areas only. While the artists had originally specified Pantone colours, the manufacturing process called for industrial paint, so the closest match had to be found.

The manufacturing process also had unpredictable results on the finely etched credits on the reverse. It was found that, despite its hard and smooth appearance, the acrylic was pitted in areas, meaning that this text would not etch as cleanly as was hoped. This problem varied from sign to sign.

In keeping with the associations with archiving, storage and transportation of artworks that *Noting Absence* makes, Blessmann and Saville chose to present these signs in cardboard archive boxes of the type commonly used by museums and libraries. Archive boxes were made especially for the signs, using brass (rather than silver or steel) staples as a precaution against rusting. The number of the staples might appear to be excessive, but the shape of the boxes and rigidity of the material meant that the box would spring apart if not held together in this way. Each box was also produced with an interior sleeve to protect the contents from scratching when being lifted out of the box.

IN COURSE OF ARRANGEMENT

Object removed for study purposes

Materials
Book Cloth, Flexible PVC,
Paper (Uncoated)

Processes
Binding, Die Cutting, Foil Blocking,
Lithography, Thermoforming

THE ELUSIVE TRUTH!
JASON BEARD

This oversized catalogue, designed by Jason Beard, was published for an exhibition of the work of Damien Hirst at the Gagosian Gallery in New York. It was originally conceived as a relatively simple book, but as the project developed it was realized that it would not be ready for the exhibition's opening, and it became something of an artwork in itself, created with few creative or budgetary compromises. The catalogue was further augmented by the publication of 500 special editions (not featured here). The project commenced in February 2005, with the last delivery of books taking place in April 2006.

The text was printed lithographically, utilizing a number of high-quality uncoated paper stocks. Given that the book was printed in Canada and designed in the UK, there needed to be a high degree of understanding and collaboration between all parties. The global availability of the preferred paper stocks helped minimize the time taken to specify the insides, thus a similar route was later taken when selecting the book cloth.

One of the major obstacles to be overcome was the image registration on the die-cut pages. The binding of the book was done by hand, thus it would have proved difficult to control this positioning throughout the binding process. Die-cutting, gluing and sewing tests were completed across all the pages. These tests showed the printer the adjustments in the processes that were needed across each section. It was decided to make use of a relatively small eight-page section to maximize the accuracy and give better control. The application of the thermoformed panel to the front cover also needed accuracy, as well as the employment of the correct adhesive to bond it securely. All the images have been glued or tipped into the text pages. Placing them in the text, prior to binding, had previously been considered, but this made the catalogue unstable and difficult to handle and sew.

Response to this project was very positive within the printing fraternity; outside of the industry it is now extremely collectible, both as a Damien Hirst catalogue and as a beautifully produced example of graphic design.

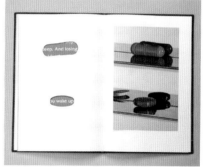

708

020 7723 8010
concierge@byindividualappointment.com

NIKEiD™

Materials
Book Cloth, Coloured Paper

Processes
Binding, Foil Blocking, Screen Printing

NIKE ID DOSSIER
BABY

Baby is an art direction and creative design agency that specializes in music, fashion and lifestyle. This project was the UK execution of the Nike iD programme whereby selected guests were invited to a specially created venue in London to design and fashion their own pair of Nike shoes. Baby created membership and referral cards to allow entrance to the venue, and a dossier cover to contain all the documents relevant to a customer's design consultation. The key emphasis was to imbue every facet of the project with a sense of luxury and premium detailing. This was reflected in the choice of venue (a town house in Mayfair), through to its interior design, also handled by Baby, and the collateral associated with the project.

1000 copies of the dossier were produced. Certain materials and processes naturally lend themselves to this type of project, for instance die stamping and foil blocking. A lot of leather and dark colours were to be employed in the interior and, for a brief moment, leather was considered for some collateral items, and for the dossier in particular. However, it had to be dismissed for budgetary reasons.

Most of the creative decisions were made on presentation of previously printed examples that demonstrated all of the substrates and manufacturing methods. This established the core of the project, with these ideas being slightly modified. The choice of an off-white stock was made in order to maximize the bright white of the foil blocking. A deep-black card could have been used for the membership card, but, again, a paler black made the black foil blocking stand out more. The reverse of both the membership and the referral cards were screen printed and sequentially numbered for identification.

Invitees completed their design consultation and were each handed a wallet containing their unique shoe design. This was then wax sealed in an envelope and placed in the dossier. The envelope was intentionally supplied without a gummed closure, as this allowed the user to open the envelope by peeling off the wax seal rather than breaking it—the spine of the dossier had to be constructed in such a way that it did not gape from the bulkiness of the wax. The envelope for the invitation was custom-made, with a much deeper flap to allow for the fleur-de-lis logo device, and to give a more elegant finish.

The project and its collateral took on a life of its own. Nike iD became one of the most desirable events to be invited to, and the dossier has become a highly coveted object in its own right.

Materials
Book Cloth, Grey Board, Metal, Paper
(Board; Uncoated), String, Wax

Processes
Die Cutting, Etching, Foil Blocking,
Rigid Box Making, Screen Printing

TG24, 24 HOURS OF THROBBING GRISTLE AND TG+
PETER CHRISTOPHERSON, COSEY FANNI TUTTI, CHRIS CARTER AND PAUL A. TAYLOR

The aim of this project was to create a CD version of a set of live recordings by the group Throbbing Gristle. The original version was released as a very short run on 24 cassettes, packaged in a leather-like flexible PVC cassette attaché case. Also housed in the box were postcards, badges and other ephemera.

The idea of re-releasing the recordings had been around for many years. There had been numerous conversations, but the demands of the job had prevented the proposal moving forward. Throbbing Gristle is very thorough about recording all its live events, and the task of re-mastering all 24 hours of recorded material would be a very onerous one. A facsimile version of the original box was devised, but the band was not happy with the results.

The eventual solution was a rigid box with a black foil-blocked hinged lid. The grey colour used was selected for its connection to the band's existing palette of colours and the box was left deliberately unlined, exposing its construction. The diversity of the elements made it a very challenging project to work on—everything had to have a very specific feel. A material for the certificate was chosen only after a rigorous assessment of many stocks. The other printed items were randomly placed within each box, ensuring that no finished piece was the same. The choice of these objects was based on what was in the original box, and gusseted envelopes to house the items were specially made, with the supplier wax-sealing them by hand.

The idea behind the stainless-steel and brass cards in the alternative *TG+* version of the packaging was to play around with the band's logo, allowing the viewer to configure the order to create different logos. The steel was photo-etched with screen-printed varnish highlights, creating very sharp detailing.

In an age where the packaging of music is often not regarded as important, Throbbing Gristle has created music packaging that, based on the current market, shouldn't work. The band's anti-commercial attitudes lead them to invert the record industry's beliefs of how music should be marketed and sold. The band even imposed the additional hurdle of releasing these recordings on Boxing Day—the release date and value did not hinder the boxes selling out in a very short space of time.

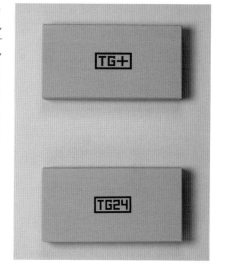

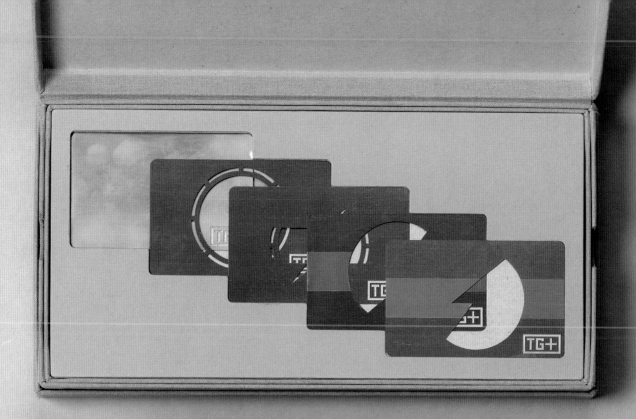

Materials
Coloured Paper, Grey Board, Paper
(Uncoated)

Processes
Binding, Die Cutting, Embossing,
Inks, Lithography

D.V.D.V.D. (DISNEY VISUAL DIGITAL VIDEO DISK)
HIDEKI INABA DESIGN

Hideki Inaba founded Hideki Inaba Design in 1997. From 1997 to 2001 he was art director of design magazine *+81*. He now works as art director for the Gas Book series and for *SAL* magazine in Japan.

The Disney DVD package documents the creation and application of a Disney store in Tokyo, following numerous Japanese designers as they create products for the store. The level of detail these designers applied in their work is followed through in Inaba's intricate packaging, which was presented to a selection of special customers.

The package consists of two trays, one housing the DVD and the other housing a brochure, both of which are inserted into an open-ended coloured-paper sleeve that has been embossed with fine type. The two inner trays comprise of a die-cut sandwich of grey board, which is covered in a printed sheet. The carrier slides neatly and effectively into each sleeve, giving easy access to the contents—the initial idea came from old five-inch floppy disks, coupled with an imagined disk from a science-fiction movie. This latter notion carried itself through to the choice of materials, and the iridescent-ink finish of the sleeves in particular.

What makes the packaging stand out particularly is the die-cut circle, which is the same size, and has been designed to lie in the same position, as the hole in the centre of the DVD (the hole is also cut through the brochure). A great deal of care has been taken to ensure that the holes are all the same size and line up perfectly. On first inspection, it is easy to forget that the DVD already has a hole in the middle, and the package gives the illusion of a magic trick, making you want to pick it up and look at it more closely.

Inaba had worked with this supplier before, and his idea could be explained easily. A great number of mock-ups and prototypes were produced to ensure that the mechanism worked effectively. The ink employed on the two inner sleeves changes colour in light, and had to be specially imported to Japan for the project. Other ideas had been considered, including the use of a thermoformed plastic—this was rejected as too costly, and because of its impact on the environment.

The packaging's design was found to be easily transferable to automated manufacture—it rests on a very imaginative use of a simple process, and on extremely accurate production. It also reinvigorated Inaba and his staff in their firm belief that inventive packaging can still be designed, developed and produced in an environment that is retracting from anything unusual.

Materials
Book Cloth, Coloured Paper,
High-Density Foam, Magnets

Processes
Closures, Foil Blocking,
Rigid Box Making, Routing

MAKRI JEWELLERY PACKAGING

SPIN

Spin is a London-based design agency set up by Tony Brook and Patricia Finegan. Ileana Makri is a jeweller based in Athens, Greece. She makes diamond and gold jewellery for a select group of customers, and asked Spin to create packaging that was appropriate for her exclusive brand.

Four boxes were created in total. The boxes were produced in three different dimensions to accommodate various sizes of jewellery, and the lining colour differs with each size, as does the size of the logo. The construction of the boxes is based on a Japanese incense box—such boxes are closed with a loop of ribbon and a piece of ivory shaped into a clip, which slides into the loop.

A magnetic strip has now replaced this arrangement, as a neat and more practical solution. Both the client and designer wanted the magnetic strip to be obscured underneath the binding material; however this would have meant a loss of magnetism and made the production of each box very time-consuming and expensive.

The selection of a material to cover the boxes was principally directed by the colour of the foam tray. A graphite black foam was the closest match to the black of the chosen colour palette, and a powdery matt-black polyurethane-coated binding material was selected for the cover. This was also a close match to the flexible PVC pouch used to house the jewellery in the box. Black foil blocking was favoured over a debossed logo as it increased legibility.

The construction of the box is similar to the case cover of a hardbound book. The foam tray is mounted in open section and the cover wraps around its shape, leaving the sides exposed. This is the detail that makes the box unusual—but it could also expose a technical problem with the foam. To achieve the depth of the recess, the foam would have to be layered then routed, which would create an unsightly line, making the box appear clumsy. To get over this problem, the deepest box had to be made from a thicker block of foam.

The end result is a set of boxes that is chic, glamorous but still extremely understated. They make a perfect setting for the jewellery housed within.

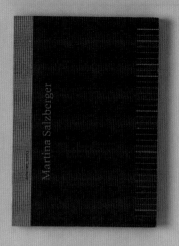

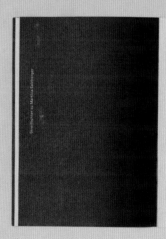

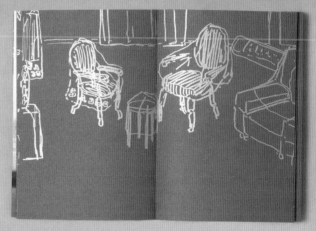

Materials
Coloured Paper, Paper
(Coated; Uncoated)

Processes
Binding, Lithography

MARTINA SALZBERGER: ARBEITEN
INGO OFFERMANNS

Ingo Offermanns is a German-born freelance graphic designer who has worked since 1999 in Germany, the Netherlands, Belgium and the USA, working for cultural clients including the Rijksmuseum, Amsterdam, and the Gutenberg-Museum, Mainz. In 2005 he designed an artist's monograph for the German artist Martina Salzberger. The book employs a number of paper stocks, together with lithography and binding, in order to distinguish the various aspects of Salzberger's practice as well as to deal with budgetary restrictions in an intelligent and innovative way.

Offermanns's challenge in responding to the commission was to find a way to represent Salzberger's very diverse, multimedia work (which takes in performance, photography, sculpture, writing and drawing) in a logical fashion. His solution was to demarcate the artworks by medium and identify each with a paper stock. A central 40-page section is printed full colour on coated paper, while the surrounding sections use a combination of one-colour printing and coloured and plain stocks, including the use of a silver ink. By the use of different colours, weights and textures of paper stocks, Offermanns added pace and avoided the impression of a mainly black-and-white book despite having only one full-colour section.

The book is bound with an open spine to further remove it from more traditional approaches to artists' monographs and to give the impression of a loose compilation of material—a further nod to the diversity of Salzberger's artistic practice.

Offermanns also wanted to invest the book with object-like status in order to combat any notions of flimsiness associated with its small size and distinguish it from a 'booklet' format. Thus he printed ink on the top side of the book block, encouraging unconventional handling of the book on the part of the reader, and investing it with a sculptural feel.

The problems Offermanns encountered during the multi-faceted production of this book were largely to do with the way the different papers responded to ink. He had planned to print the first and last eight-page sections with a Pantone grey, but the paper reacted unexpectedly so the printer used a four-colour grey instead. Another problem was the ink on the upper side of the book block. The different paper stocks reacted variously to the ink, absorbing it at different rates and causing pages in some sections to tend to stick.

On the whole, this innovative approach to the design of an artist's monograph is a success story and demonstrates how close attention to conventional printing processes and careful paper selection can reinvigorate a traditional medium.

Material
Coloured Paper (Board)

Process
Thermography

MARC ATLAN DESIGN, INC. BUSINESS CARD
MARC ATLAN DESIGN, INC.

Marc Atlan has worked with Tom Ford, Rei Kawakubo, Oliver Stone, Helmut Lang and others, creating perfume packaging, art directing ad campaigns, conceiving T-shirts and building installations.

For a designer, designing and producing your own corporate stationery can be difficult—it throws up myriad possibilities, as there are few or no restrictions on the materials and processes that are available to you, and there is no brief imposed by an external client. It's extremely important to get it right—all your potential customers and peers will see it, and if you can't get your own stationery right, it will not inspire people's confidence in you as a designer.

The striking black-on-black business card that Marc Atlan decided upon uses thermography, a process that is economical to use and cost-effective for low print runs (only 250 cards were produced). He was not particularly keen on the idea of having a conventional business card; this process allowed him to create something that was understated but still intriguing.

The selection of a black uncoated board coupled with the glossy, textured thermographic ink created a tactile yet subtle solution—it has also been purposely designed so that you cannot write on it. The card minimizes the 'orange peel' effect that some people find unappealing about the thermographic process. In addition, the card's thickness and the texture of the ink are together very satisfying

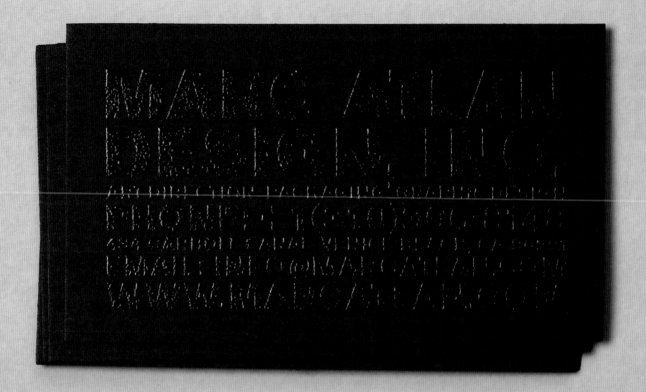

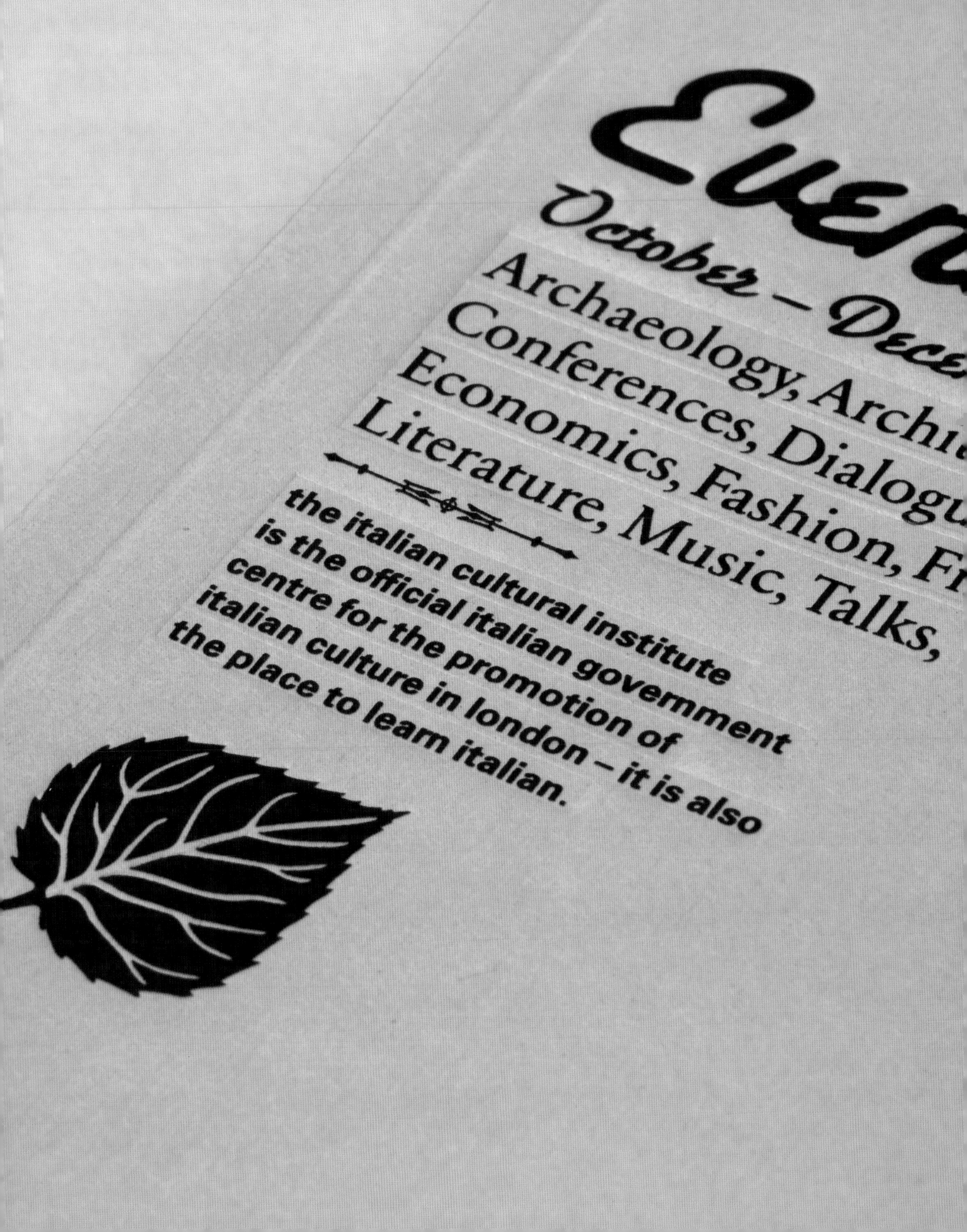

Eventi

October – December

Archaeology, Archi
Conferences, Dialogu
Economics, Fashion, Fi
Literature, Music, Talks,

the italian cultural institute
is the official italian government
centre for the promotion of
italian culture in london – it is also
the place to learn italian.

THE ITALIAN CULTURAL INSTITUTE

Events

October 2005 – January 2006

Architecture, Art, Conferences, Dance,
Design, Dialogues, Film, Gastronomy,
Italian Language, Literature,
Music, Photography, Talks, Theatre.

the italian cultural institute
is the official italian government
centre for the promotion of
italian culture in london – it is also
the place to learn italian.

THE ITALIAN CULTURAL INSTITUTE

Events

February – May 2006

Architecture, Art, Conferences, Dance,
Design, Dialogues, Digital Art,
Economics, Fashion, Film,
Gastronomy, History, Italian Language,
Literature, Music, Philosophy,
Photography, Poetry, Talks, Theatre.

the italian cultural institute
is the official italian government
centre for the promotion of
italian culture in london – it is also
the place to learn italian.

THE ITALIAN CULTURAL INSTITUTE

Events

June – September 2006

Architecture, Art, Classics, Conferences,
Dialogues, Digital Art, Economics,
Fashion, Film, Italian Language,
Literature, Music, Talks, Theatre.

the italian cultural institute
is the official italian government
centre for the promotion of
italian culture in london – it is also
the place to learn italian.

THE ITALIAN CULTURAL INSTITUTE

Events

October – December 2006

Archaeology, Architecture, Art, Classics,
Conferences, Dialogues, Digital Art,
Economics, Fashion, Film, Italian Language,
Literature, Music, Talks, Theatre.

the italian cultural institute
is the official italian government
centre for the promotion of
italian culture in london – it is also
the place to learn italian.

Materials
Coloured Paper, Paper
(Coated; Uncoated)

Processes
Binding, Embossing, Lithography

ITALIAN CULTURAL INSTITUTE LONDON PROGRAMME
BRIGHTEN THE CORNERS

Brighten the Corners is an independent, multi-disciplinary design and strategy consultancy, with offices in London and Stuttgart, established in 1999 by Frank Philippin. In 2005 they were asked to create a series of small brochures for the Italian Cultural Institute, London, that were to outline the events taking place there each quarter.

The pocket-sized guides are perfect bound with coloured covers, which are printed in a single colour and then embossed. Different paper stocks are used within to give the project more depth and contrast. The guides open with a series of atmospheric photographs shot in various Italian cities, which are printed on a coated cream stock. The purely typographical listings element of the programme is printed in black on an uncoated recycled stock. Typography is kept simple throughout, each new month is marked with a black page, and there is a small grey section at the back detailing events held outside the Institute.

Using contrasting stocks proved a very economical way of creating literature that had a tactile quality and, at the same time, felt more expensive than it actually was. The only problematical element in the production process was ensuring that the strength of the embossing on the cover was correct—embossing on different coloured stocks was found to result in slightly different impressions.

The guides were very popular with visitors to the Institute—the feedback was that users found the guides understated and pleasing to use. They show that information design doesn't have to be dull or unattractive—the guides are modest yet covetable objects that beg to be picked up and looked through.

Materials
Corrugated Cardboard, Paper
(Flock; Uncoated)

Processes
Binding, Carton Making, Lithography,
Screen Printing

365: AIGA YEAR IN DESIGN 24
COMA

COMA comprises designers Cornelia Blatter and Marcel Hermans, with bases in Amsterdam and New York. They act as art directors for Dutch magazine *Frame*, and also collaborate on projects ranging from art and photography to publishing and product design.

Every year the American Institute of Graphic Arts (AIGA) holds an awards scheme, which aims to gather together all the best American graphic design of the year. The selected work is published as an annual, which is then sent out to members and sold to non-members.

The factors that made this edition of the annual unique are its fairly modest size and the fact that it is a softback, which makes it portable—more like a guidebook or a manual. Most design annuals are grandiose hardback affairs that will never leave the studio and feel like a conclusion rather than part of a series.

Another element not found in most annuals is the stream of consciousness piece written by Nicholson Baker early one January morning. This text starts on the front cover and flows on to the first two pages. There are two more instalments mid-book that are printed on orange pages, and the piece concludes on the back cover. These pages also act as an additional navigational device. The designers chose this text as they felt its mundane quality echoed the everyday nature of graphic design, and that its insights and curiosity resonated with the enquiring outlook of most designers.

Because of the amount of material involved, the priority for the designers was to create a navigation system that would be very simple to use. There is a table of contents at the beginning, as well as at the front of each section, and the page number, project number, title, category and designer appear on the bottom of each page.

In contrast to the relative restraint of the insides, the cover features a tactile flock paper with a velvet-like texture, transforming perceptions of the annual from book to object. The text is reversed out in white and hard to ignore—it is the first thing you read and becomes the book's title. The actual title appears along the bottom of the cover, mirroring the navigation system inside.

The cover stock would not survive too much handling on a bookshelf, so the designers took the very practical step of giving the book its own custom-designed screen-printed box, which is made from corrugated cardboard. As well as protecting the book, it also served as ready-made packaging for the copies that were sent out to AIGA members.

COMA's sensitive treatment of the source material, combined with an imaginative use of materials, give this project a life of its own, transcending the traditional, stuffy awards brochure.

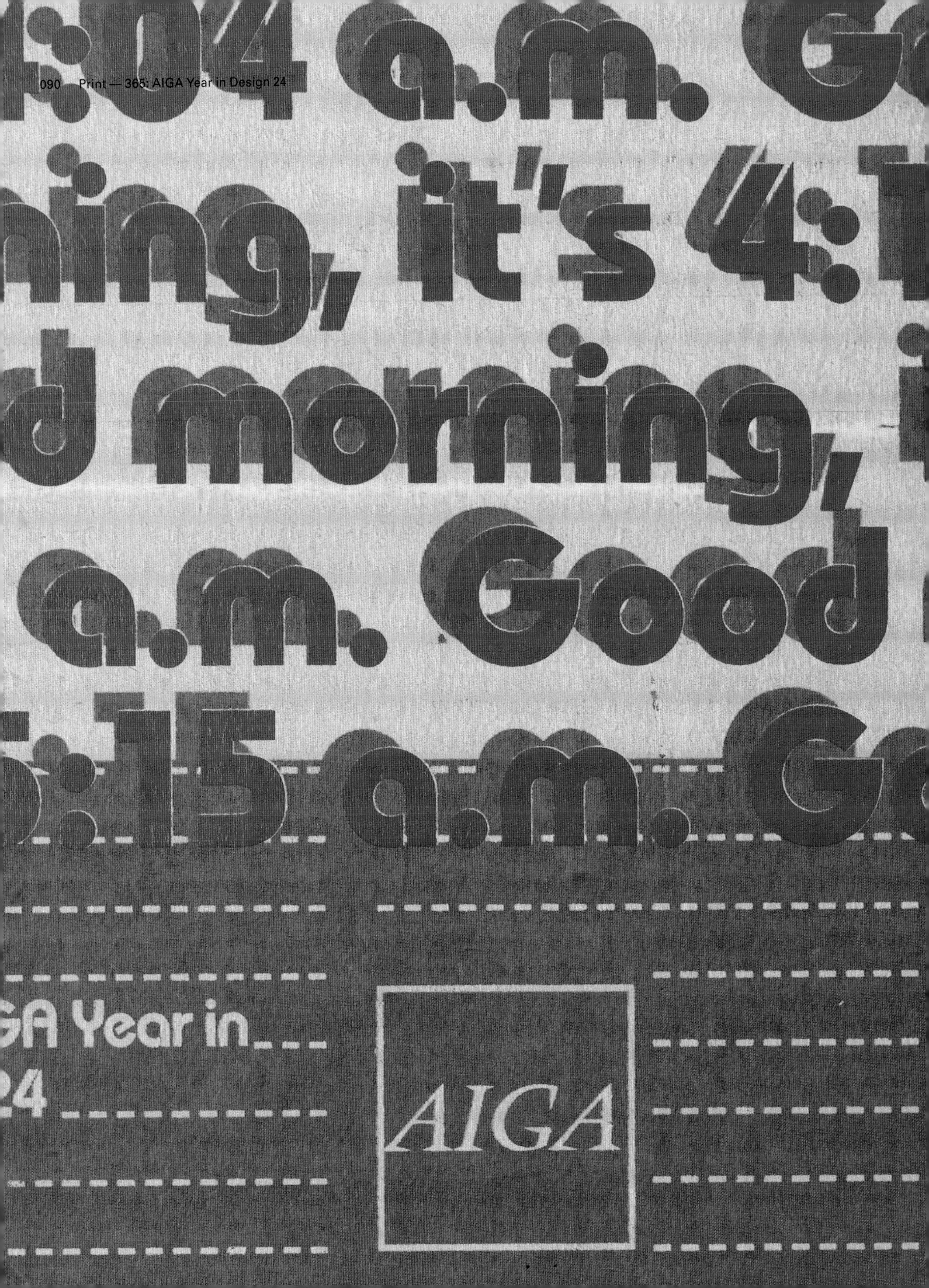

:04 a.m. Go

ning, it's 4:1

d morning,

a.m. Good

:15 a.m.. G

GA Year in

24

AIGA

Good morning, it's January and it's 4:17 a.m., and I'm going to sit here in the dark. I'm in the living room in my blue bathrobe, with an armchair pulled up to the fireplace. There isn't much in the way of open flame at the moment because the underlayer of balled-up newspaper and paper-towel tubes has burned down and the wood hasn't fully caught yet. So what I'm looking at is an orangey ember-cavern that resembles a monster's sloppy mouth, filled with half-chewed, glowing bits of fire-meat. When it's very dark like this you lose your sense of scale. Sometimes I think I'm steering a spaceplane into a gigantic fissure in a dark and remote planet. The planet's crust is beginning to break up, allowing an underground sea of lava to ooze out. Continents are tipping and foundering like melting icebergs, and I must fly in on my highly maneuverable rocket and save the colonists who are trapped there.

AIGA

American Institute of Graphic Arts

It's 4:17 a.m.

365: AIGA Year in Design 24

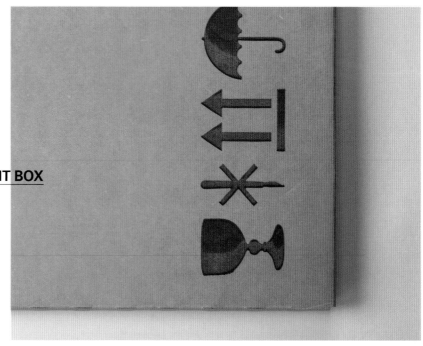

Materials
Corrugated Cardboard, Low-Density
Foam

Processes
Die Cutting, Flexography

DAMIEN HIRST PRINT TRANSIT BOX
[N/A]

This box was commissioned by Paul Stolper Gallery to protect limited-edition silk-screen prints by the artist Damien Hirst in transit when they are sent around the world via courier. As well as offering a high degree of protection for these valuable items, the boxes needed to look good. A sample in Stolper's possession provided the idea for an execution that achieved the former, without also requiring a separate solution to ensure an attractive container.

The box is made up of three elements: the outer box, an inner box and also a foam panel. All the elements perform specific tasks that interconnect to provide protection for the prints. The outer box is made from a twin-walled brown corrugated cardboard material, which is given greater strength by using a thicker top sheet and a thicker layer between the two gauges of flute.

As the box is quite shallow and the material very thick, a perforation instead of a crease is used to allow it to roll together. Adhesive foam tape is also employed, as ordinary double-sided tape would not have been sufficiently strong. Velcro was considered as a method of closure as this would allow the recipient to open and close the box many times, but this was not regarded as essential and was discounted early on in the project.

The box is printed flexographically with hazard symbols that were specially modified by the artist. Screen printing would have produced a sharper and more opaque print, but, as well as being very expensive, ultimately it was not possible because of the large sheet size required.

The inner box is made from a white corrugated material with the direction of the flute running opposite to the flute direction of the outer box. When placed one inside the other, this produces an extremely rigid and inflexible package—very important given the size of the whole. The foam pad allows more than one print to be housed in the box, expanding or contracting dependent on the contents. The inner box is sealed with specially printed adhesive tape.

To ensure that the box would work, 20 were prototyped and posted or sent by various methods. The box has become a vital appendage to the artwork it contains, and is itself collectible.

Materials
Corrugated Cardboard, Felt, Paper
(Board; Coated), White Board

Processes
Foil Blocking, Lithography,
Screen Printing

GE IMAGINATION NOTEBOOK
GIAMPIETRO+SMITH

Giampietro+Smith is a New York-based design studio. Founded by Rob Giampietro and Kevin Smith, its work focuses on cultural, editorial and non-profit projects for clients such as Princeton Architectural Press, Knoll, *The New York Times* and the United Nations. They created the Imagination Notebook for contract publisher Melcher Media, which had been commissioned by General Electric (GE) to produce a promotional piece to be used as a holiday gift.

To mirror the book's theme of imagination, the cover is formed from white board (manufactured by GE), allowing the user to draw their own cover as many times as they wish. A covered corrugated outer box was printed with Thomas Edison's original sketch for the light bulb—this box houses the book, along with a branded dry-erase marker and a felt bookmark which can also be used as a cloth with which to wipe the cover. The book itself includes handwritten thoughts on innovation from GE's engineers and notable inventors, as well as sketches from famous notebooks including those of Frank Gehry and Piet Mondrian.

The materials used are highly varied, as are the processes, which all conspires to create a considered and complete project with an outer packaging that becomes as vital as its contents. The book tape, which holds the text together on the bound edge, has been foil blocked, and the white boards and the bookmark are screen printed.

The designers had a very specific sense of which materials and processes would be appropriate—the biggest challenge was to find a white-board material that would not dent or chip at the corners. The book was originally intended to have square corners, but these were found to be uncomfortable to handle. As well as being easier for the reader, it was felt that the radius corners made the item seem more like the notebook it was intended to be.

It would have been easier to produce a more traditional leather-bound book, stamped with gold foil, echoing GE's engineering notebooks, but a forward-thinking solution was considered more appropriate to the brand. The more inventive approach paid off—when the Imagination Notebook was presented to end-users it was voted a resounding success.

Re-Shuffle/
Notions of
an Itinerant
Museum

FROM

TO

Center for Curatorial Studies
Bard College, PO Box 5000
Annandale-on-Hudson, NY 12504-5000

RE-SHUFFLE: NOTIONS OF AN ITINERANT MUSEUM
is a project wherein forty-seven cultural producers consider the possibilities of
a mobile, reactive museum. This exhibition-as-publication was organized by first-year
students in the master's degree program at the Center for Curatorial Studies
at Bard College, New York (CCS). We encourage you to re-shuffle it and pass it on!

Published on the occasion
of Re-Shuffle: Notions of
an Itinerant Museum, an
exhibition-as-publication,
organized by Markús Thór
Andrésson, Kirin Buckley,
Max Hernández Calvo,
Özkan Cangüven, Ruba Katrib,
Florencia Malbrán,
Kate McNamara, Laura Mott,
Rebeca Noriega-Costas,
Amy Owen, Chen Tamir,
and Emily Zimmerman,
first-year students in
the master's degree
program at the Center for
Curatorial Studies, Bard
College. The
publi...

Published by
Center for Curatorial
Studies, Bard College
P.O. Box 5000
Annandale-on-Hudson,
NY 12504-5000
www.bard.edu/ccs/exhibitions
reshuffle@bard.edu

EDITOR
Damian Da Costa

DESIGN
Project Projects,
New York

Printed in G...
by Ka...

The Museum Within:
Taking the proposal for an itinerant museum
as an inquiry into how to live a life

Museums, residences of the muses, are
repositories of conserved art. No matter
how often... that sense becomes a vehicle to promote
the necessity to trust one's inherent... level and acknowledge the shift from
...

RE-SHUFFLE: NOTIONS OF AN ITINERANT MUSEUM
is a project wherein forty-seven cultural producers consider the possibilities of
a mobile, reactive museum. This exhibition-as-publication was organized by first-year
students in the master's degree program at the Center for Curatorial Studies
at Bard College, New York (CCS). We encourage you to re-shuffle it and pass it on!

PARTICIPANTS	LOCATIONS	OCCUPATIONS
Vito Acconci	Akureyri, Iceland	Adjunct curator
De Appel Curatorial	Amsterdam, The Netherlands	Architect
Training Programme	Barrytown, NY	Art critic
Julieta Aranda	Belo Horizonte, Brazil	Artist
Magali Arriola	Bogotá, Colombia	Artist collective
Dean Baldwin	Boston, MA	Assistant professor
Davide Balula	Bratislava, Slovakia	Associate professor
Judith Barry	Brooklyn, NY	Chief curator
François Bucher	Buenos Aires, Argentina	Cultural producer
Dan Cameron	Cali, Colombia	Curator
Anetta Mona Chisa	Carpinteria, CA	Curatorial archivist
& Lucia Tkacova	Hagersten, Sweden	Curatorial students
Papo Colo	Hannover, Germany	Designer
Danger Museum	Helsinki, Finland	Director
Köken Ergun	Istanbul, Turkey	Educator
Verónica Fatule	León, Spain	Independent curator
Harrell Fletcher	Lima, Peru	Graphic designer
Gabriel Fowler	London, England	MA candidate
Amy Franceschini	Los Angeles, CA	Painter
Christophe Gallois	Lugarno, Switzerland	Photographer
Sandra Gamarra	Milan, Italy	Professor
Ragnheidur Gestsdóttir	Madrid, Spain	Researcher
Gabriela Golder	Mexico City, Mexico	Senior curator at large
Hlynur Hallsson	Munich, Germany	Visual anthropologist
Pablo Helguera	New York, NY	Writer
Sasha Huber	North Adams, MA	
& Petri Saarikko	Oslo, Norway	
Pepe Karmel	Paris, France	
María Angélica Melendi	Portland, OR	
Gian Paolo Minelli	Rotterdam, The Netherlands	
José Miyashiro	San Francisco, CA	
Gerardo Mosquera	São Paulo, Brazil	
Joseph Nechvatal	Tokyo, Japan	
Eric Tinlup Ng	Toronto, Canada	
Pepon Osorio	Verdun, Canada	
The Partners		
Pavilion Projects		
Gastón Pérsico		
& Cecilia Szalkowicz		
Libia Pérez de Siles		
de Castro		
& Ólafur Árni Ólafsson		
Tatjana Myoko von Prittwitz		
Rosamond Purcell		
Red 76		
José Roca		
Agustín Pérez Rubio		
Regina Silveira		
Laurel Sparks		
Christopher Sperandio		
& Simon Grennan		
Dannielle Tegeder		
Nato Thompson		
Måns Wrange		

The Museum You Want
http://www.icaboston.org/
Home/Media/ArtistWebProjects

CURATORS
Markús Thór...
Kirin Buckl...
Max Hernánd...
Özkan Cangü...
Ruba Katrib...
Florencia M...
Kate McNama...
Laura Mott...
Rebeca Nori...
Amy Owen...
Chen Tamir...
Emily Zimme...

<u>Materials</u>
Coloured Paper, Corrugated Cardboard,
Paper (Board; Gummed; Uncoated)

<u>Processes</u>
Carton Making, Lithography, Screen
Printing

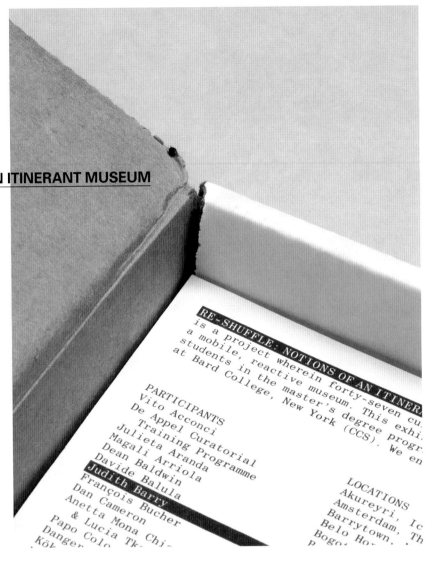

RE-SHUFFLE: NOTIONS OF AN ITINERANT MUSEUM
PROJECT PROJECTS

Project Projects was set up in 2004 by Prem Krishnamurthy and Adam Michaels, producing environmental, interactive and print design for the cultural sector. In addition the New York-based studio produces a range of independent projects including lectures, publications and events. This piece saw the studio collaborate with 12 first-year MA students at the Bard College Center for Curatorial Studies in New York. The concept behind *Re-Shuffle: Notions of an Itinerant Museum* was to circumvent the traditional methods of interacting with art in a gallery setting, placing work directly in the hands of viewers and asking them to create their own unique version of the exhibition. This required an approach to the materials that would allow for each work in the exhibition to function as an independent object, as well as fitting a format that would link it to the exhibition as a whole. It would also need to be fully portable and mailable.

The designers chose to present the exhibition as a set of cards, housed in a standard hinged-lid transit box, which they screen printed with the show's title. They also designed a special mailing sticker for the recipient's address. The curators gave a brief to 47 artists and writers, asking them to respond to the notion of 'the contemporary relevance of cultural institutions'. Each participant's contribution was printed on a square piece of card. These varied from photographs, illustrations and texts, to strip cartoons, collages, puzzles and stickers. An exhibition of the work was held at Art in General in New York; visitors were encouraged to assemble and take away their own portable version in the boxes provided.

As well as portability, economy was an important factor in the designers' choice of materials—Project Projects conducted extensive research into a variety of formats. They also wanted to create something that would emulate the artistic reference points for the project. All materials were chosen for being inexpensive and aesthetically pleasing, and were intended to have a roughness and informality that would reference the show's 1960s conceptual-art antecedents. The result is a simple and effective solution that allows the viewer to fully interact with this imaginative collection of artworks.

Materials
Corrugated Cardboard, Flexible PVC,
Mirri-Board, Paper (Kraft; Glassine;
Tracing)

Processes
Binding, Die Cutting, Embossing,
Foil Blocking, Inks, Lithography,
Screen Printing

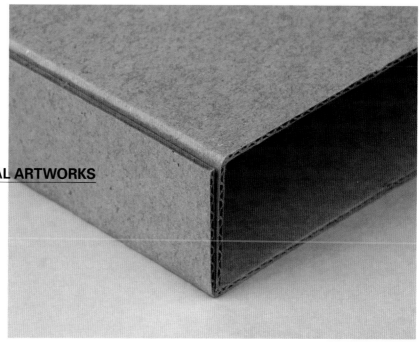

THE SHADOW OF THE OFFICIAL ARTWORKS
MO'DESIGN INC.

Mo'design Inc. was established in 2000 by Motoki Mizoguchi, and specializes in magazine and fashion design for the Japanese market. *The Shadow of the Official Artworks* comprises a summary of the design work of DJ-turned-designer Hiroshi Fujiwara. There are two versions: one with a white cover for foreign markets and the other with a black cover for the domestic market. 999 copies of each were printed, with the same text common to both versions.

The book's slipcase is made from die-cut corrugated cardboard. The lightning-bolt device could only be die cut from a very fine-fluted corrugated board to achieve the points of the bolts. It also allows the user to see which version they own. The book is covered in a matt-laminated paper with gloss UV-varnished text over the top. It is interesting to note that both matt lamination and UV varnish will always differ, dependent on which country an item has been printed in. It always seems that processes have a superior result in Japan than that in any other country—in the case of lamination, a Japanese finish always feels smoother and less synthetic, and in the case of varnish, to have a greater density.

When you turn the cover, you might expect to see a thread-sewn book. However, because of the diversity and random use of stocks, along with the number of tip-ins, the book has been perfect bound. From this point onwards the text is classified by its subject: artworks, graphic logos, CD jackets, T-shirts, enterprises and collaboration with brands. Various materials and processes differentiate one area from another.

UV varnish was used to pick out the detail of the logos, as its density has a finish more akin to thermography. White foil blocking was used to create a hand-painted effect for a sweatshirt graphic, while lithography was employed on mirri-paper for a collage later in the text. This double page has a tendency to curl—this could be due to the binding or the deposit of ink on the mirrored surface. There is also cockling on the plastic sheets that make up the CD jacket designs, but this does not detract from the finished product.

The die-cut tracing paper, backed with a recycled kraft packing paper, adds yet another material, technique and dimension. This is followed over the next few pages by early T-shirt graphics printed on kraft paper to give them a nostalgic feel. A base white has been printed first to allow for the intricacy of the designs, ensuring that they are legible on the page. Further on in the book, parts of a logo have been screen printed with a reflective ink, while each copy has been numbered on the last page, with a small sheet of glassine paper overlaid. The only difficulty noted by the designer was deciding which material and process would be most appropriate for which section.

The book is an amalgam of printing processes that are rarely seen together in one printed piece. It is a beautiful book to handle and use and, considering the number of print treatments contained within its pages, does not feel excessive. The work of Hiroshi Fujiwara is marked by a peerless attention to detail—his approach and work methods are mirrored here.

UNDERCOVER
JUN TAKAHASHI
featured by
W.W.

communion w

Materials
Felt, Paper (Card; Coated; Uncoated),
Polyethylene

Processes
Binding, Flexography, Lithography

UNDERCOVER JUN TAKAHASHI FEATURED BY W.W.

COMMUNION W

The Hong Kong-based design studio
Communion W was set up in 1998 specializing in graphic design for advertising and
the music industry. As well as its commercial
practice, the studio produces an annual
publication—*W.W.* Each edition tells the
story of a creative person who has inspired
the Communion W team and their creative
director, Joel Chu. In 2004 they published
Undercover Jun Takahashi Featured by W.W.,
dedicated to the radical Japanese fashion
designer Jun Takahashi.

A homage to Takahashi, the volume
is a visual documentary of Communion W's
evolving relationship with the designer and
also a record of his thoughts and philoso-
phies. The journey begins with Communion
W's visit to Takahashi's Undercover Lab in
Tokyo in 2003 and continues on to Paris to
witness his Spring/Summer collection on
the catwalk in autumn 2004. It also includes
specially commissioned contributions by
other artists, responding to Undercover.

The publication was printed as an
edition of 4000. The perfect-bound book
comes enclosed in a black felt dust jacket,
with an embroidered clothing label as its title
panel, which directly references the book's
fashion content and creates a tactile link
between book and subject. It is packaged
in a flexo-printed polyethylene bag.

Four different paper stocks, from
coated to uncoated, are used for the book's
interior, with the texture and printing surface
of each paper specially chosen to reflect
the qualities of the imagery. Thus a section
of illustrations is printed on a lightweight,
textured paper, while atmospheric black-
and-white abstract photographs are printed
on a glossy stock. Compromises were made
in the selection of paper stocks and the
thickness of the felt because of budgetary
constraints. The result is still a highly original
visual biography that reflects the ingenuity
and maverick stance of its subject.

Materials
Concrete, Grey Board, Magnets

Processes
Casting, Closures, Rigid Box Making

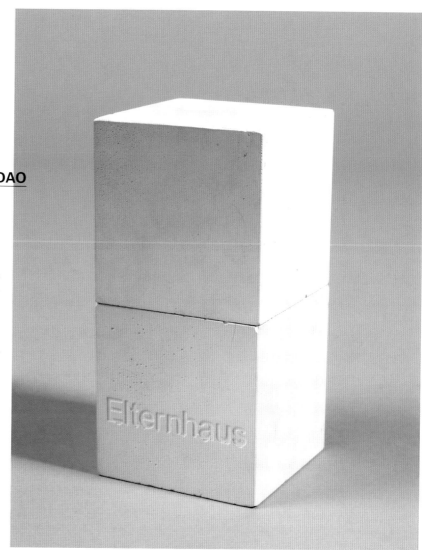

MOSLBUDDJEWCHRISTHINDAO
ELTERNHAUS

Elternhaus was created as a specific company to produce this perfume and its packaging. Founded by Daniel Josefsohn (a photographer) and Susanne Raupach (an architect) they have handled all design, press, advertising and production for the project. 300 units were created in total.

The principles surrounding the project are bound up in a number of philosophical chains of thought. Perfume is a multi-layered essence; therefore it can be read as something sensual, religious or political. The name was born as a result of the events of 9/11 and a wish for all religious hostility to cease. The white colour of the packaging signifies peace, and the hard surface with its debossed logo signifies religious precepts chiselled in stone. The packaging's weight reflects the gravity of the theme.

The packaging that houses the glass perfume bottle is made of self-compressing white concrete. This material also contains white quartz powder, glass fibre, water and a plasticizer; it was a by-product of the black concrete formulated for Peter Eisenman's Holocaust memorial in Berlin. The packaging is like a piece of sculpture—pleasingly heavy and extremely smooth. The most satisfying feature is the way the two halves click firmly together, thanks to the invisible magnets embedded in the concrete.

There wasn't a great deal of money to invest in a more automated manufacturing process, so everything was moulded by hand. Fortunately, Raupach already had experience of pouring concrete for building architectural models while she was at college. The finished packaging is polished with sandpaper, sprayed with a transparent varnish and then polished again to create the smooth finish.

Porcelain had been considered at one stage, along with a lining for the bottle recess. However, the raw version was preferred. The designers also liked the faults in the concrete—the packaging subverts current accepted notions of how perfume should be presented. The product, which has proved highly successful, does not directly seek to challenge beliefs; rather it aims to explore ideas. The end result is in stark contrast to the glossy and polished executions of the larger fragrance manufacturers.

Elternh

MARK BUXTON
DANIEL JOSEFSOHN
TETJUS TÜGEL

pour

Elternhaus.

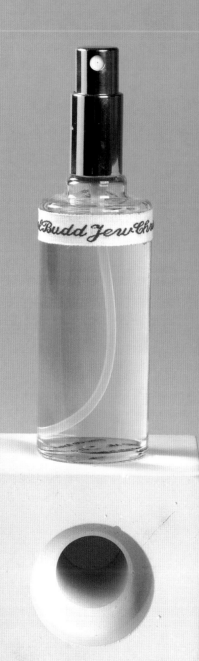

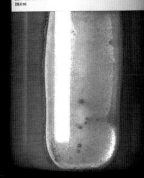

KRINK.

KRINK is premium quality silver ink.
Permanent on any surface.
Handmade in NYC.USA.
Unfadeable.

Directions:
Shake well until thoroughly mixed
Shake well between applications.

R11; Flammable. R20/21 Harmful by
inhalation and in contact with skin.
S16; Keep away from sources of ignition-
No smoking. S24/25; Avoid contact with skin
and eyes.

Keep out of reach of children. Contains
petroleum distillates. Do not ingest

FOUR U.S. OUNCES
118 ml.

KRINK.

KRINK is premium quality silver ink. Permanent on any surface.
Handmade in NYC.USA.Unfadeable. **Directions:** Shake well until
thoroughly mixed. Shake well **between applications.**
Warning: R11; Flammable. R20/21 Harmful by inhalation and in contact with
skin. S16; Keep away from sources of ignition- No smoking. S24/25; Avoid contact
with skin and eyes. Keep out of reach of children. Contains petroleum distillates.
Do not ingest.
EIGHT U.S. OUNCES
236.6 ml.

NEW YORK CITY, U.S.A. 2002

Materials
Book Cloth, High-Density Foam, Magnets

Processes
Closures, Foil Blocking, Rigid Box
Making, Routing

KRINK INK
ALIFE

This packaging was created for the
New York-based store and creative hub, Alife,
with all manufacture taking place in the UK.
The intention was to create a luxury package
to house a product—a brand of ink called
Krink Ink, developed and manufactured by
the New York graffiti artist KR—that would
not normally be presented in this way.

There were a number of highly complicated components in the box—it houses
a bottle of silver ink and a 'mop', enabling
you to write with it, as well as four spare
nibs. A card tray would not have housed
them efficiently and would have looked unsightly, so a routed high-density foam block
was produced. This allows the items to be
inserted and removed easily, and prevents
the contents from falling out when the box
is displayed in an upright position.

The black cloth-bound box was the
obvious choice to give the desired level of
exclusivity to the ink. However, it needed
to have a contemporary feel and be capable
of being presented at point of sale. The box
is quite deep, so it would have been difficult
to open if it had a lift-off lid because of the
resulting vacuum. A hinged lid was selected, along with a magnetic-strip closure.

The silver foil-blocked Queens logo
on the front of the box had to fall off the
foot of the lid like paint dripping—this posed
problems when the box was covered, and
a high degree of accuracy was required. The
foiling was done before the box was covered
—this meant there was no debossed effect
in these areas. In retrospect, the selection
of cloth was possibly not the best decision,
as the foiling did not take particularly well
to the surface. However, it was felt that the
cloth gave the nicest finish and colour and,
once signed by KR, the product gave every
impression of the luxury item that it was
intended to be.

Materials
Book Cloth, High-Density Foam, Magnets

Processes
Closures, Foil Blocking, Rigid Box
Making, Routing

KRINK INK
ALIFE

This packaging was created for the
New York-based store and creative hub, Alife,
with all manufacture taking place in the UK.
The intention was to create a luxury package
to house a product—a brand of ink called
Krink Ink, developed and manufactured by
the New York graffiti artist KR—that would
not normally be presented in this way.

There were a number of highly complicated components in the box—it houses
a bottle of silver ink and a 'mop', enabling
you to write with it, as well as four spare
nibs. A card tray would not have housed
them efficiently and would have looked unsightly, so a routed high-density foam block
was produced. This allows the items to be
inserted and removed easily, and prevents
the contents from falling out when the box
is displayed in an upright position.

The black cloth-bound box was the
obvious choice to give the desired level of
exclusivity to the ink. However, it needed
to have a contemporary feel and be capable
of being presented at point of sale. The box
is quite deep, so it would have been difficult
to open if it had a lift-off lid because of the
resulting vacuum. A hinged lid was selected, along with a magnetic-strip closure.

The silver foil-blocked Queens logo
on the front of the box had to fall off the
foot of the lid like paint dripping—this posed
problems when the box was covered, and
a high degree of accuracy was required. The
foiling was done before the box was covered
—this meant there was no debossed effect
in these areas. In retrospect, the selection
of cloth was possibly not the best decision,
as the foiling did not take particularly well
to the surface. However, it was felt that the
cloth gave the nicest finish and colour and,
once signed by KR, the product gave every
impression of the luxury item that it was
intended to be.

Materials
Acrylic, High-Density Foam, Paper

Processes
Binding, Foil Blocking, Lithography, Routing

TABOCA PRESENTATION BOX
THE KITCHEN

London-based design agency The Kitchen was established in 1999. It specializes in design, art direction and packaging for clients including Levi Strauss, Habitat and Speedo. They have also worked with Taboca AS, a Scandinavian company that produces luxury snus.

Snus is a form of tobacco, a little like moist snuff, that comes in small pouches and is ingested by being placed beneath the lip. This product is popular in Sweden and Norway, where Taboca AS identified a gap in the market for a high-end luxury snus, which would use the kind of premium-grade tobacco produced for fine cigars. After signing a licensing agreement with Cuban cigar manufacturers Habanos to utilize tobacco from the Montecristo and Romeo Y Julieta brands, Taboca's next step was to produce a package to present and explain these products to potential buyers.

The new packaging needed to be both elegant and contemporary, thus the designers chose the colourway that is most often associated with Habanos—black and gold. An initial idea for the project was to produce a wooden box similar in style to a cigar box, but this was soon discounted as being too traditional. Later a polypropylene sleeve was prototyped but was not deemed elegant enough. Eventually the final configuration was prototyped—a black heat-bent acrylic sleeve with a repeat pattern of the Taboca, Romeo Y Julieta and Montecristo logos foil blocked in gold.

Foil blocking had always been the designers' choice for printing the repeat logo, but until a visit to a foil-blocking company it had been assumed that it would not be possible to get the foil to adhere to an acrylic surface. However, having persevered with this option, the final results, say The Kitchen, 'are stunning'. Within the slipcase, four tins of snus are housed in a casing of high-density foam. They are accompanied by a 24-page saddle-stitched booklet printed lithographically on a highly reflective, glossy black paper stock with a cover of deep-black rubberized board. These two stocks, together with the ingenuity of the packaging, create a dynamic contrast of textures that compounds the designers' aim to devise a contemporary take on luxury cigar packaging that would energize the high-end snus market.

Game Components

1 Game board
40 Game cards
4 Game pieces
1 Die

Game Setup

Place the board on a flat surface and the shuffled game cards face-down in one pile. Each player chooses one game piece to represent them on their travels around the board.

Gameplay

Players begin at the flagship store at 301 Oxford Street, spend the night out in London, and eventually arrive at the final square representing 'home'. The object of the game being to be the last remaining player on the board, as they would have enjoyed the best evening out.

Each player in turn throws the dice and moves their game piece forwards the number of spaces indicated. Following on from this, they should then pick up a game card and do as it describes.

This involves moving forwards and backwards a number of squares, which is expressed in terms of good and unfortunate events that might occur on a night out on the town. The card should then be returned face-down to the bottom of the deck. The next player should then take their turn.

Among the game cards are some rogue cards that allow for one player to effectively sabotage the evening of any other player of their choice. This involves sending the other player forwards a designated number of squares. The player who plays the card benefits by moving back a number of squares as designated. These cards should be played immediately as with the other cards.

Once a player has reached the final square representing their home, they are out of the game. The other players should resume play as before, until one player wins the game and declares their place.

Rules

Players must always roll the dice and travel forwards the number of squares as indicated by the dice, before picking up a card. Players should always pick up a card after rolling the dice. This card must be played immediately. Players should only travel forwards, unless otherwise indicated by the card.

Once a player has reached the final square they have finished the game, even if they are halfway through their turn and are yet to pick up a card.

If the situation should arise at any point during the game where a player doesn't have enough spaces to move back, they should just return to the starting square (301 Oxford Street).

Mitchell has a table for you at The Ivy next to Sting, take three steps back and enjoy your meal.

301 Oxford Street, London.

RIVER ISLAND

RIVER ISLAND   A limited edition of 100.

301 Oxford Street, London.

Materials
Acrylic, Book Cloth, High-Density Foam,
Paper (Board), Velvet

Processes
Foil Blocking, Rigid Box Making, Routing,
Screen Printing

RIVER ISLAND GAMES BOX
SATURDAY

This project was produced as a press gift for the UK fashion retailer River Island to launch its flagship store on Oxford Street in London. An innovative press gift was required in lieu of a launch party (which tends to be the preferred method for fashion events). London-based design agency Saturday came up with the idea of a board game about going out in London, with the winner being the one who manages to stay out the longest. All of the questions reflect insider knowledge of London's nightlife. This was designed to reflect River Island's position as a brand people wear to go out.

The initial specification hinged on whether the acrylic material used for the board could be supplied thicker than the usual 3mm, a standard gauge for this material from stock. The decision to use black as the palette for the project allowed for a 10mm acrylic to be sourced from stock—black, white and clear are shades that tend to be more readily available given their use in signage and display applications. It was also fortunate that enough material was already available at the manufacturers without having to be ordered. To maintain the high degree of finish, each panel was flame polished on the edges to create a finish that was as smooth as the top surface. Flame polishing, however, changes the surface of the material, causing print to craze, or not print at all, where heat has been applied. The print area had to be calculated to ensure the maximum size of the game-board design. The design itself was screen printed in a matt black.

The box itself is a rigid box with a flange on the base. This means that when the lid is placed on the base they form a seamless cube. The lid has been foil blocked with a metallic black foil that sets off the fine weave of the cloth. A black-faced board has been employed to minimize the cost of lining the box.

The foam tray is made from black foam, as opposed to the more commonly available graphite-coloured material. In this instance, a more expensive, anti-static foam was used, its darker appearance owing to the introduction of carbon. This also makes the foam softer and velvety in texture. The velvet bag uses a silk tassel drawstring closure and houses the gaming pieces, which are fabricated from glow-edge acrylic. A number of shapes were considered and trialled for these pieces, the handbag shape being the most difficult to realize.

The cards and box were printed on the same sheet with 100 per cent black and a high-build varnish to pick up the decorative pattern, which took at least two days to dry fully. The project was well received, with *Women's Wear Daily* calling it the best press gift ever.

Materials
Book Cloth, Fabric, Mirri-Board,
Paper (Cardboard; Uncoated)

Processes
Binding, Lithography, Rigid Box Making,
Screen Printing

WHAT'S GOOD? BOOK AND DVD SET
ALLRIGHTSRESERVED LTD

AllRightsReserved Ltd (ARR) is a Hong Kong-based studio working across the fields of design, publishing and event management. It has curated and organized a range of exhibitions and conferences, among them the What's Good? Conference.

The first of its kind, this conference in Hong Kong brought together speakers at the top of their field across the creative industries, including Droog Design, Kazunari Hattori, John C. Jay, Martin Margiela and Peter Saville, each of whom spoke about the core principles of what drives excellence in their particular practice. A limited edition of 200 commemorative book and DVD sets designed by ARR was made to document the event, using photographs and artwork by the speakers, excerpts from their presentations and a filmed version of the entire four-day event. A conference guide and DVD case were cloth bound and housed in a second, similarly cloth-bound slipcase. Each item was silk-screen printed with the set's contents information. Additionally, a larger hardback volume documenting the work of the speakers was produced, which came in its own thick, black, button-fastened bag made of cotton.

The extensive use of cloth binding posed several challenges for the designers, requiring a lot of research and experimentation to account for the absorbency of the papers. The cloth edges are cut flush to the board on which the cotton is mounted, thus exposing edges that are left unprotected, producing a frayed finish. This was one aspect of the production that it was difficult to control, but ARR feel that the packaging benefits from the frayed edges becoming coarser over time.

The overall effect of the finished product is of a simple but very finely fashioned presentation set. This hand-crafted feel is balanced by very high production standards —some abstract conference photographs were finished with a pale beige varnish as a subtle touch—and the package would seem an apt answer to the question posed in the conference's title, 'What's Good?'.

Day 1_____//:/: John

_ _ _ _ _ _ _ _ //:/: Kashiwa Sato_ _ _

_ _ _ _ _ //:/: Kaikai KiKi Co., Ltd._ _ _

_ _ _ _ //:/: groovisions_ _ _ _ _

//:/: Droog Design _ _ _ _ _ _

Day 2_____//:/: Peter

_ _ _ _ _ _ //:/: Christopher Doyle_

_ _ _ _ //:/: Yugo Nakamura_ _ _ _ _

//:/: Maison Martin Margiela_ _ _ _

Day 4_____//:/: Kazu

Hattori_ _ _ _ //:/: colette_ _ _ _ _

:: book

What's good?
DATE:8-11TH JAN, 2005 CONFERENCE
*Arts and Creativity Festival @Hong Kong Arts Centre

What's good?
DATE:8-11TH JAN, 2005 CONFERENCE
*Arts and Creativity Festival @Hong Kong Arts Centre

Janvier
Digital lab
65, rue de Dunkerque
75009 Paris, France.
T + 33 (0) 1 53 20 22 00
F + 33 (0) 1 53 20 22 09
Email janvier@janvier.fr
www.janvier.fr
Janvier
Digital-Lab
65, rue de Dunkerque
75009 Paris, France.
T + 33 (0) 1 53 20 22 00
F + 33 (0) 1 53 20 22 09
Janvier
Isabelle Decamps
65, rue de Dunkerque
75009 Paris, France.

Materials
Paper (Coated Board), Polythene,
Self-Adhesive

Processes
Flexography, Lithography

JANVIER DIGITAL LAB IDENTITY
LAURENT FÉTIS

Laurent Fétis is a designer and art director based in Paris with a broad spread of clients in the music and fashion industries. Janvier Digital Lab is one of the most famous photo retouching companies in Paris, with a reputation for high-end work with luxury brands and advertising clients. It has also been instrumental in promoting emerging creative talent and magazines, leading to Janvier developing its own imprint, publishing books by artists and photographers.

Fétis was contacted by the owners of Janvier with the idea of changing its logotype and identity. One concern was that the existing identity relied heavily on photographic executions, which were dependent on collaborations with clients. It also tied Janvier down to certain styles that became subject to the vagaries of fashion, thus leaving the identity looking out of date quickly. The conclusion was to create some enduring collateral material that was both practical and also desirable enough for the end-user to want to keep it.

The bulk of the pieces are printed conventionally. It is the polythene envelope that is the key component in this family of items, as this is the piece of collateral that the client interacts with the most. The envelopes are fabricated from a heavy gauge of polythene to mimic the type of envelope that photographic paper is usually supplied in—this also serves to protect the contents. In addition, a cardboard liner was printed to keep everything flat. Its graphic was printed on a big sheet at as large a scale as possible then trimmed, ensuring that each liner would be different when removed from the envelope. A clear space was left on the envelope for the application of mailing labels (or handwritten details). This graphic was employed across all press advertising, and a different design is planned each year.

Fétis sourced the best manufacturers and prices exhaustively to keep the job within budget. What started out as a simple rebranding exercise has transformed the company's identity, making it instantly recognizable both to its clients and beyond in the wider world.

Material
Paper (Uncoated)

Processes
Binding, Lithography

BELOW THE FOLD JOURNAL
WINTERHOUSE INSTITUTE

Below the Fold is published by William Drentell and Jessica Helfand, partners in Winterhouse, a design studio focusing on publishing and new-media projects for cultural institutions. The pair are co-founders of design blog Design Observer and have published books under their own imprint.

Below the Fold is a self-initiated project first published in autumn 2005. Sent out free to those requesting it from their website, in each issue various contributors set out to explore a single topic, examining ideas that are 'below the fold'. Its creators intend the narrative to reveal alternative ways of looking at the world around us. The journal appears irregularly: two issues have been published so far, covering the topics 'Journals' and 'Danger'.

The 16-page broadsheet is printed on a quality uncoated stock that resembles newsprint paper but gives a far superior printing surface. The journal is saddle stitched and then folded in half widthways.

Because of the relatively small print run of 2000, the designers had originally planned to print using web off-set (a method commonly employed to print newspapers), but this process did not give the quality that was required. The solution was to go back to basics—the project was reformatted and the more traditional sheet-fed litho print process was substituted, this time with excellent results.

The minimal design, modest stock and two-colour process serve to reinforce the journal's spontaneous, handout feel. All the images appear in greyscale, with overprinting used to add texture, employing a strong colour such as red or green. This juxtaposition of the highbrow content with the somewhat lo-fi aesthetics makes for an engaging and vigorous publication.

VOLUME 1. NUMBER 2. Warning. Danger. Caution. Anxiety. Fear. Terrorism. Poison. Biohazard. Accident. Emergency. Crime. Bomb. Attack. Catastrophe. Disaster. Plague. Once remote and loosely suggestive, these words have come to be an integral part of our modern lexicon, daily reminders of the inevitability of fear, the persistence of assault, the frailty of everyday life. It is the potential for terrorism — not just the unspeakable act itself — that has become so meaningful in our time. It is also a deeply shared truth, our incapacity to comprehend boldly premeditated violence on such an epic scale. How does the practice of design even begin to accommodate such a phenomenal shift in social and political needs? From poison labels to warning tapes to staged disasters to computer viruses, we dwell in a world of elevated suspicion. Concrete security bollards masquerade as park benches. Banned materials circumscribe even the most innocent of excursions. Increasingly, the material evidence of prevention seems inversely proportionate to its effectiveness. As we learn to better anticipate and filter catastrophe on local and global scales, our perceptions relocate themselves within alternate contexts — some personal, others spiritual, and all of them deeply visual. The quest for security has now repositioned itself at the core of our lives. This issue of Below the Fold: explores the artifacts of modern anxiety, the emotional response to fear, the narrative arc of disaster, and the visual language of caution, prevention and security. What does it mean to be safe — and will we know it when we are? FALL 2005.

VOLUME 1. NUMBER 1. Literary panoramas. Political stalemates. Historical standards. Material Obsolescence. Topics that fly below the radar yet persist nonetheless, shifting perspectives and sparking debate. This is the purview of Below the Fold: — an occasional publication from the Winterhouse Institute that adapts classic journalistic paradigms through the critical lens of visual inquiry. Where do we turn when leadership is compromised? What do we understand when we look at literary and scientific journals? Why is the human hand so frequently at odds with the man-made? When is photographic evidence a smokescreen for truth? How do we determine directions, distinguish messages, decode the landscape, divine the future? Within the limitations of a printed publication, each issue of Below the Fold: will explore a single topic through visual narrative and critical inquiry, examining ideas that are technically "below the fold" to reveal alternative ways of looking at the world we live in. From a forgotten muralist of the twentieth century, to the media doublespeak of the twenty-first, to the questionable veracity of political jargon, to the visual language of third-world cultures, we will explore the visual permutations of modern life. In this, our premiere issue, we look at the virgin efforts of scholarly journals — an editorial genre perhaps best characterized by its arcane and often impenetrable content. Yet in spite of their extraordinary topical range, what these publications share is an unparalleled idealism, a sense that the future holds nothing but opportunity and promise. — The Editors. SPRING 2006.

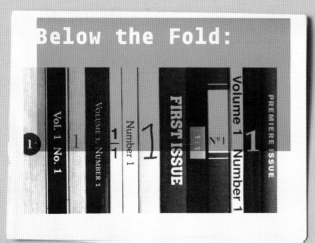

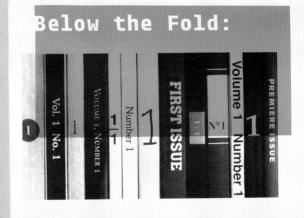

Literature &
Politics

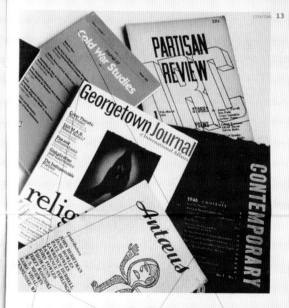

ANG
GABi
K.A.i.
MAMi
PAPi
YOURs

PRO-
DUCED
WITH
LOVE
AT
FUTURE
PLANET
OF
STYLE
MADE
IN USA

DRY
CLEAN
ONLY

PRO-
DUCED
WITH
LOVE AT
FUTURE
PLANET
OF
STYLE

MA-
CHINE
WASH
TUMBLE
DRY

WWW.
ASFOUR.
NET

PRO-
DUCED
WITH
LOVE AT
FUTURE
PLANET
OF
STYLE

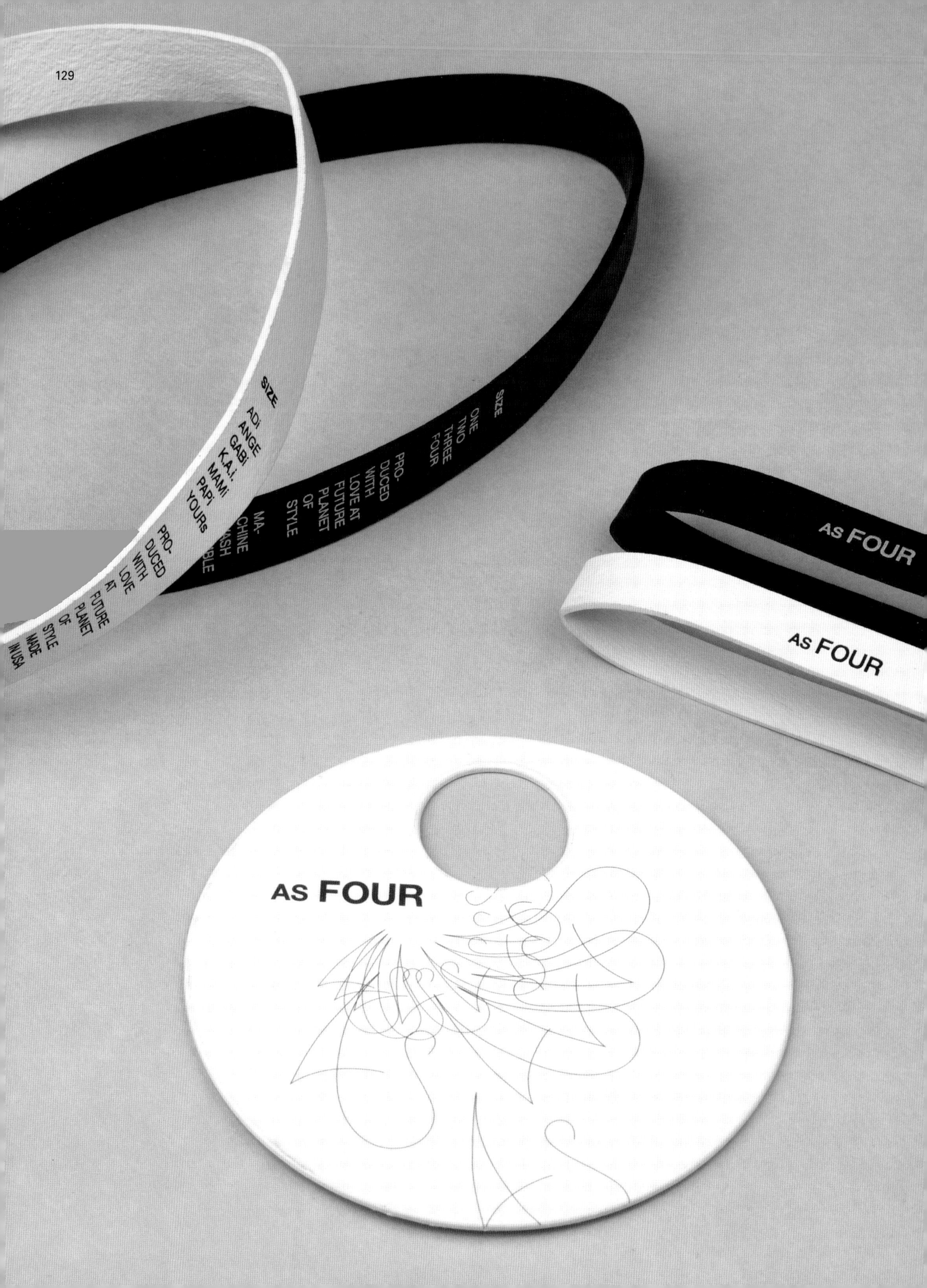

SIZE
ADi.
ANGE
GABi.
K.A.i.
MAMi
PAPi
YOURS
MA-
CHINE
WASH
UNABLE
PRO-
DUCED
WITH
LOVE
AT
FUTURE
PLANET
OF
STYLE
MADE
IN USA

SIZE
ONE
TWO
THREE
FOUR
PRO-
DUCED
WITH
LOVE AT
FUTURE
PLANET
OF
STYLE

AS FOUR

AS FOUR

AS **FOUR**

Materials
Coloured Paper, Rubber Bands

Processes
Die Cutting, Foil Blocking, Lithography,
Screen Printing

THREEASFOUR IDENTITY
STILETTO NYC

Stiletto nyc is a design studio based
in New York and Milan, founded by Stefanie
Barth and Julie Hirschfeld. It creates print
and motion graphics for a diverse range
of clients. Stiletto has been working with
THREEasFOUR—a New York-based fashion
collective—since 2004.

Stiletto was responsible for creating
the company's original identity, which was
loosely based on flowing Arabic script. Since
then Stiletto has created various seasonal
look books and fashion-show invites. The
format for the invites changes every season
but stays true to the minimalist aesthetic
that runs through the clothes. So far the
invites have included a four-colour folded
poster, a folded black-and-white poster, a
black card silk-screened with light-grey ink,
a card printed with copper ink, and a white-
on-white debossed card made by letterpress
with no ink. While Stiletto were excited by
the result of this last experiment, they felt
that it was perhaps slightly too subtle.

The most ambitious invitation to date
has been a curvy, die-cut card printed with
metallic gold ink. The striking, fluid shape,
which mirrors the company's identity, has
delicate flowing lines and several curved
cut-out sections in the centre.

Stiletto was also commissioned by
THREEasFOUR to create a range of in-store
clothes tags. The resulting round, die-cut
clothes tag, with its cut-out circle, is a neat
solution that also happens to mirror the
shape of a bag that appeared in their Spring/
Summer 2006 collection. In addition to this,
Stiletto sourced black and white industrial
rubber bands, which were screen printed
with every clothing size.

The rubber band and tag are looped
together with black thread, allowing the
individual size to be marked off on the band.
Both are hung from the clothes hanger, giving a striking, cost-effective solution that
remains in keeping with THREEasFOUR's
cutting-edge approach.

Material
Paper (Bond)

Processes
Black-and-White Printing, Hand Folding

RUMORS
MORALITY OF OBJECTS

Jiminie Ha is co-founder of New York-based design studio Morality of Objects, which specializes in creative direction and design across architecture, interiors, print and motion work. She is also editor of online architecture forum Archinect.

This self-initiated project was devised to explore ideas about conversational language—about gossip, secrecy and, as the title indicates, rumours. Ha's starting point was phrases used in the type of spoken dialogue where gossip or salacious information is passed on—'Between you and me' and 'Check this out', for example. These phrases provided the starting point for a series of posters. Each aspect of the posters' physical production was informed by this concept, as Ha explains: 'I linked [the production] to childhood memories of passing notes in class, and the elaborate methods we had of folding these notes.'

Ha established a number of grids based on different paper-folding configurations—a paper aeroplane, a triangle and an envelope. Different elements of cut-up and folded paper were then scanned to create whole designs. These were then printed on a black-and-white printer to create the posters, which were finally trimmed and folded. The type on the posters seems to whisper conspiratorially out from a black background, emulating the secrecy that surrounds the conversations transcribed.

The only problem that Ha encountered was the white border produced by the printer, because 'such printers don't print full bleed'. She overcame this by accounting for the border in the composition of the cut-up forms during scanning.

The posters prompt further thoughts about how to explore relationships between spoken words and typographic words—how phrases used in the private arena can be publicly displayed, and how that tension could be exploited.

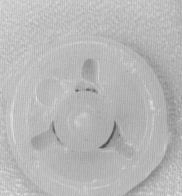

RYOJ.
MORT
1 HEADPHONICS [
2 LSDS
PRODUCED AND P
APRIL 15, 1998.
AVONDEN". THAN
STAALPLAAT, P.O.
NETHERLANDS. P.
SLEEVE BY ALOREN

YOUR NUMBER:

Material
Polypropylene

Processes
Closures, Die Cutting, Screen Printing

RYOJI IKEDA, MORT AUX VACHES SERIES
ANGELA LORENZ

Angela Lorenz is a designer based in Berlin and Vienna. Her practice, alorenz, has worked mainly for musicians and record labels, but has also created print work for publications, music festivals and cultural institutions, as well as devising live visuals for performances at festivals, conferences and universities.

One of her longest standing collaborations is with Amsterdam's Staalplaat Records, for which she has designed sleeves for the label's Mort Aux Vaches series. For a CD by Japanese musician Ryoji Ikeda, Lorenz devised a unique polypropylene sleeve. Ikeda's experimental approach to electronic composing consistently pushes sound technology to its limits. The materials and processes for the Mort Aux Vaches sleeve are directly influenced by the music. 'The music is 100 per cent synthetic and it sounds it,' explains Lorenz. 'Part of it is meant to be listened to on headphones and experiments with the spatial perception of sound versus the sonic perception of space … paper would not have been appropriate for this kind of stuff, which is why we chose to use polypropylene.'

The CD was produced as a numbered limited edition of 1000 and is at once very simple and complex in its construction. The basic structure is a panel of polypropylene, scored and folded three times. The CD sits in the central section; the sides fold into this section and are held together with a white plastic nipple fastened though the central hole of the CD and the holes punched in the plastic. The CD itself is printed with a pattern of fine, concentric, closely spaced lines. The pattern is repeated on the central section of the sleeve, and when the two are moved against each other a moiré effect is created. The polypropylene is smooth on one side and textured on the other. It can prove a difficult material on which to print, and it was a struggle to find an ink that would adhere, but eventually the printers managed to find an old pot of discontinued ink that worked.

Material
Rigid PVC

Process
Injection Moulding

THE BRICK
HUGH BROWN

As creative director of Rhino Records, Hugh Brown is in the enviable position of being able to create high-production-value record packaging with both a close attention to detail and innovative usage of material and process.

This pack houses all of the albums by Talking Heads, collected into one box. There had been a previous Talking Heads box set—*Once in a Lifetime*—but this release was different, as it marked the first time that all of the band's material had been made available as a digitally re-mastered box set. Given the difficulty of choosing a title that everyone liked, its shape and feel led to the project being referred to as 'The Brick' from an early stage.

The principle was to put as many song titles as possible on the outside of the box in a bid to create a sculptural object with a monolithic feel. The box itself was injection moulded in the Far East. Hugh Brown had used this process before for a *Star Wars* project and it was deemed appropriate to use again, as he was already aware of its possibilities and limitations. An additional, deeper layer was required for the band's name, thus creating both raised and recessed text, rendering it almost unreadable.

At an early stage a clear version was considered, with white CD jewel cases, but this was later rejected. Most releases from Rhino contain an expanded booklet. In the case of *The Brick*, a small print accompanied each title. There was a notion to place all of these in a modified CD jewel case but one could not be found.

There were few problems dealing with a manufacturer abroad. The design was created as one flat layout. The different depths of text were indicated by creating a colour-coded chart. Brown also took the precaution of etching a metal plate which indicated the result he required.

A prototype was produced as a series of panels glued together. This was deemed very successful and only required slight modifications to the type and to ensure the correct shade of white. An extremely tight fit was requested, but this would have created a vacuum, preventing the user from removing or inserting CDs. A tiny, discreet and barely detectable hole was thus drilled into the spine to relieve the pressure—this necessity only became apparent when the prototype had been produced.

Aside from a shipping time of one month, the project took only three months to prototype and manufacture. A minor disappointment was that a clear sticker was required to label the box. However, *The Brick* is still a beautiful object to hold, interact with and display, with an appeal that extends beyond just fans of the music.

多木浩二
森山大道

THE JAPANESE BOX

多木浩二　高梨豊　中平卓馬
森山大道　荒木経惟

Materials
Coloured Paper, Paper (Card; Coated;
Tissue; Uncoated), Rubber Bands,
Self-Adhesive, Wood

Processes
Binding, Closures, Lithography, Screen
Printing

THE JAPANESE BOX
KARL LAGERFELD AND GERHARD STEIDL

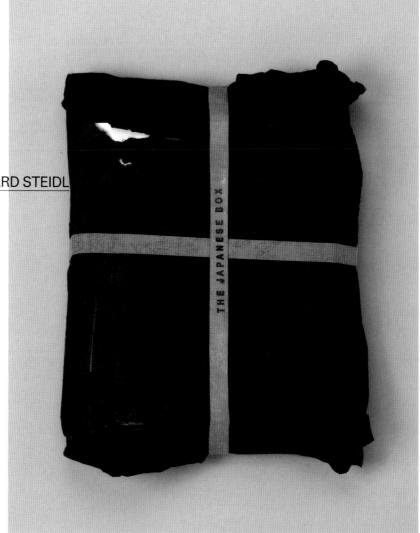

Karl Lagerfeld is often talked about as being one of the most influential fashion designers of the twentieth century: he currently has his own fashion label as well as being chief executive of design at Chanel. Once an assistant to artist Joseph Beuys, Gerhard Steidl established Steidl Publishing in 1966. The company has produced some of the most attractive books of recent years, including *The Japanese Box*, a facsimile reprint of six photographic publications from the late 1960s and early 1970s.

Included in *The Japanese Box* are three issues of the photographic magazine *Provoke*, along with *Sentimental Journey* by Nobuyoshi Araki, *Bye, Bye Photograph Dear* by Daido Moriyama and *For a Language to Come* by Takuma Nakahira. All the books deal with photography and were originally produced with essays and texts by Japanese photographers and writers whose work was a response to the climate of moral unrest in Tokyo (and around the world) in 1968. These publications benefited from massive leaps in print technology kick-started by the Tokyo Olympic Games of 1964, when the standards of lithography and photogravure rose to meet the new challenges of design and image.

The books are presented in a lacquered wooden box that has been screen printed on the lid. The box has two catches and is hinged. Inside the lid, a handwritten self-adhesive label indicates the number of the box. The books themselves are wrapped in black tissue paper held together with red rubber bands, one of which has been rubber stamped with the name of the project.

From experience, it can be extremely difficult to replicate the materials, and even the printing methods, of the past faithfully. Over the decades, technology moves on and records have been lost, making it very challenging to match the print qualities of a bygone era. And if the piece was originally printed in another country, accurate replication is almost impossible.

Each publication in *The Japanese Box* is beautifully executed, from the stock to the print to the binding. *Provoke 1* and *2* are printed in single colour on a coated stock, the extent of which is bookended with text print on a grey paper. *Provoke 3* is printed

entirely on uncoated stock with a red card cover. This harks back to its original publication in 1969 when the quality of the paper and the tone of the photographs were specifically chosen to achieve a rough finish. The resulting dot gain in the images gives them an almost silk-screen look. Despite the perfect binding, the three other titles begin to feel more like books, both in their format and in their use of plain endpapers. The whole box represents a level of detail and diligence rarely found in this type of print work.

Material
Flexible PVC

Process
Screen Printing

THE BACKPACK PROJECT POSTER
JULIETTE CEZZAR

Juliette Cezzar is the principal of the design firm e.a.d., the art director of *Res* magazine and has designed books, websites and identities for clients including *Idea,* Yale University and MoMA, New York.

In this project for Artspace Inc., a non-profit, artist-run contemporary art space in New Haven, Connecticut, Cezzar combined clear flexible PVC with silk-screen printing to create an invitation for participants in a group show entitled The Backpack Project. The premise of the project was that each of the participants would be given a clear plastic 'safety' backpack as the foundation for a piece of work. These backpacks are mandatory in many high-risk schools in the USA as an anti-gun and anti-drug measure. Cezzar's approach and use of materials emulate the concept of the exhibition—that of playing with notions of visibility, privacy and danger—while depicting the properties of the materials used in the artworks.

Cezzar took a clear backpack, filled it with water and photographed it for the main image on the poster. She then superimposed the image of a goldfish, an addition that informed the choice of colour for the posters, which were printed in one colour, a Pantone orange, on a clear 5mm flexible PVC substrate. Silk screen is the preferred method for printing on PVC and Cezzar had used it in a previous job on a more rigid plastic. In the case of The Backpack Project, flexible PVC was the more appropriate and also more practical choice, reflecting as it did the material used to make the backpacks themselves, while making the posters easy to distribute in tubes and display in large quantities in abandoned storefronts around New Haven. It was printed as an edition of 500 posters.

The only problem Cezzar encountered during production was a slight loss of image resolution that occurred as a result of the silk-screen printing. The posters elicited responses from over 200 artists, designers, teachers and students, whose broad range of reactions made for a highly successful exhibition and discussion event.

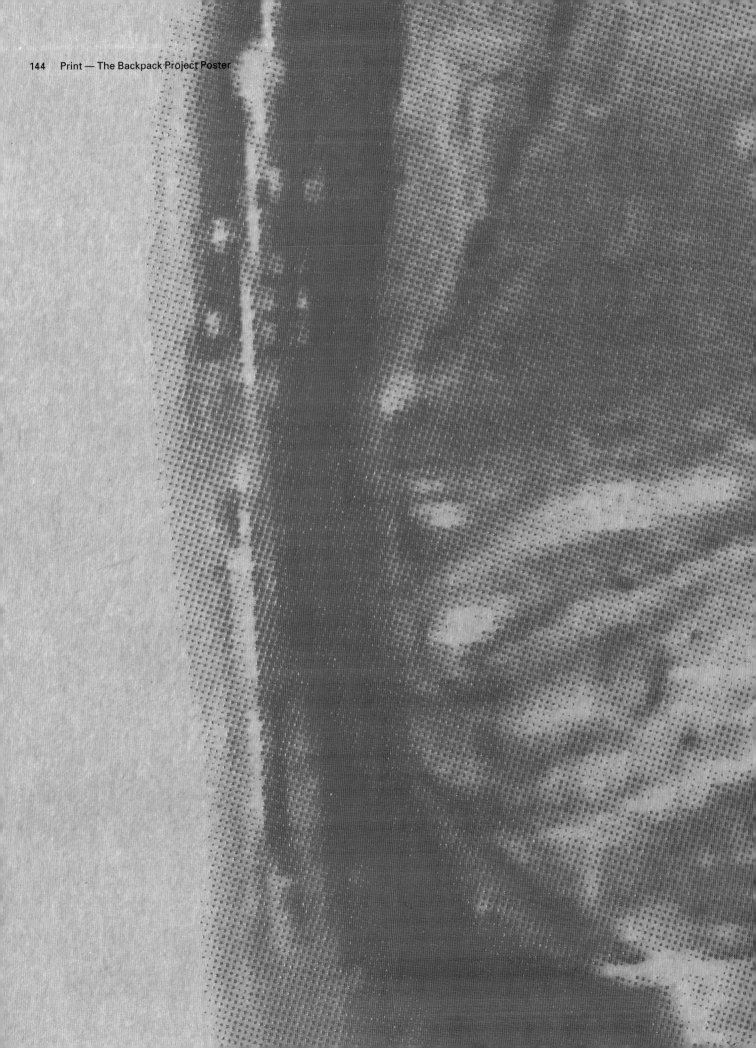

ARTSPACE invites you to participate THE BACKPACK PROJECT, a large-scale public art event and exhibition.

FILL IT, WEAR IT, JOIN US, HANG IT.

BACKPACK WEAR-IN, GATHERING, AND HANGING
Friday, June 14, 6-9 pm @ the new Artspace,
50 Orange Street (at Crown)

The exhibition will be held from June 14-30 in conjunction with the International Festival of Arts and Ideas. Backpacks will be available starting in May at ARTSPACE.

ENTRY FEES
Participation is free with a $10 deposit, to be returned when you come to the opening with your backpack. Or, if you would like one to be mailed to you, please send $15 to: ARTSPACE, 220 College Street, New Haven, CT 06510. Students and community groups: contact us if you wish to make alternative arrangements.

GUIDELINES
Collaborative packs and group efforts are encouraged. All packs are welcome at the wear-in. However, ARTSPACE reserves the right, at its discretion, not to hang any pack that it deems unsafe, or not in keeping with the community spirit of the event. In addition, our anchoring system cannot support packs over fifty pounds. Please check your weight. In order to create a unified exhibition, only the pack issued by ARTSPACE will be accepted. Feel free to call and discuss your project.
After the exhibition, backpacks can be picked up July 1-3, 12pm-6pm.

ABOUT SAFETY BACKPACKS
Safety backpacks were introduced in the wake of the Columbine High School shootings. They are now required by many high schools across the country, and promoted as an anti-gun and anti-drug measure.

ABOUT ARTSPACE
ARTSPACE fosters appreciation for the vital and dynamic role that visual artists play in our community. Its mission is to catalyze artistic activity, connect artists, audiences, and resources, and redefine art spaces.

MORE INFO
(203) 772 2709 or
derek@artspacenh.org

Many thanks to seethrubackpacks.com for providing backpacks for the event.

JUNE 14-30
THE BACKPACK PROJECT

147

Material
Rigid PVC

Process
Injection Moulding

KAWS BENDY PACKAGING
KAWS

The Kaws Bendy is unusual in the family of figures produced by this New York-based artist. The majority of Kaws figures are supplied in conventionally printed cardboard cartons, with the emphasis being on the figure itself, rather than on the total package. Recent figures have been supplied in foil-blocked corrugated boxes but, being flexible, the Bendy needed its own rigid packaging. This presented Kaws with a great opportunity to augment the new figure by experimenting with materials and processes. Kaws has a long-standing relationship with the Japanese-based toy manufacturer, Medicom—his figures are manufactured at a number of different factories, according to the finish required.

Kaws had already collected a number of injection-moulded animals by designer Verner Panton, having admired their sculptural nature, and his interest in using this process was reignited when he acquired a set of Pantone plastic colour chips. This presented him with a large new palette that it was possible to produce as plastics. The idea of creating a free-standing box to house the figure provided the final element that allowed the project to come to life.

Despite this being the first time Kaws had used the injection-moulding process, the development of the box was relatively simple, particularly as there were no expectations placed on the results. Digital files were supplied, along with a paper template for the supplier to work from. The initial prototypes provided information as to how detailed the design could be, while also revealing how the injection points could be obscured within the surface detail. First samples also showed that the weight of the plastic needed to be changed to prevent a concavity on the lid. It normally takes around six months to produce a Kaws figure, but the Bendy took eight months as a result of the extra work involved in the construction of the box.

A clear version of the Bendy was produced first, with versions in pop art-inspired colours following later. The colours of the six boxes correspond with that of the toy in each box. The plastic used for the boxes has a tendency to scratch when it is removed from its cellophane wrapping, but opaque colours are usually more forgiving in this respect. The coffin-shaped boxes also look good when stacked on top of each other. Despite the fact that some people felt that the packaging was too expensive (it was more costly to produce than the toy inside), there has been a favourable reaction to the whole product.

Material
Rigid PVC

Processes
Lithography, Thermoforming

THE/LE GARAGE POSTER
GRAPHIC THOUGHT FACILITY

Graphic Thought Facility (GTF) is a London-based graphic-design consultancy, set up by Paul Neale and Andy Stevens in 1990. Paul Elliman is an independent designer who teaches and writes for magazines such as *Fuse*, *Idea* and *Dot Dot Dot*. In 2004 GTF and Elliman were invited to take part in the annual Chaumont Poster Festival, which takes place in the town of Chaumont, near Paris. The space at which they were showing had previously been a garage, hence the title of this commemorative poster.

The poster is made from a four-colour print on a sheet of 1000-micron matt-white plastic, which was then thermoformed. This was the first time that this combination of thermoforming and four-colour print had been used by the designers, but they had been waiting for several years for a suitable project on which to use the two production methods together (GTF's way of working means that many ideas and processes are kept on the back burner, waiting for the right job). This particular combination seemed perfect for this project because the relative independence/interdependence of the two components (printing and forming) offered an opportunity for Elliman and GTF to design independently, yet together.

GTF worked with an Italian company that manufactured *trompe l'oeil*-effect point-of-sale materials and thus had plenty of experience of using both of the processes. The plastic was printed first as a flat sheet; the three-dimensional element was then thermoformed from a fret-cut MDF mould. This mould would normally be machine cut for accuracy, but the factory did not have this capability. The use of an MDF mould was a very cost-effective solution and it minimized tooling costs. This choice was assisted by the fairly modest 750 print run —a longer run would have required more expensive steel tooling.

Although at first glance this appears to be a complex project, it was relatively simple compared to the sort of item that the factory was generally asked to produce. The element that made things fairly easy was the fact that the design did not require precise registration between the print and the 3D components. As GTF are quick to point out, the hitch-free nature of this project was essentially a result of dealing with the correct supplier for the job.

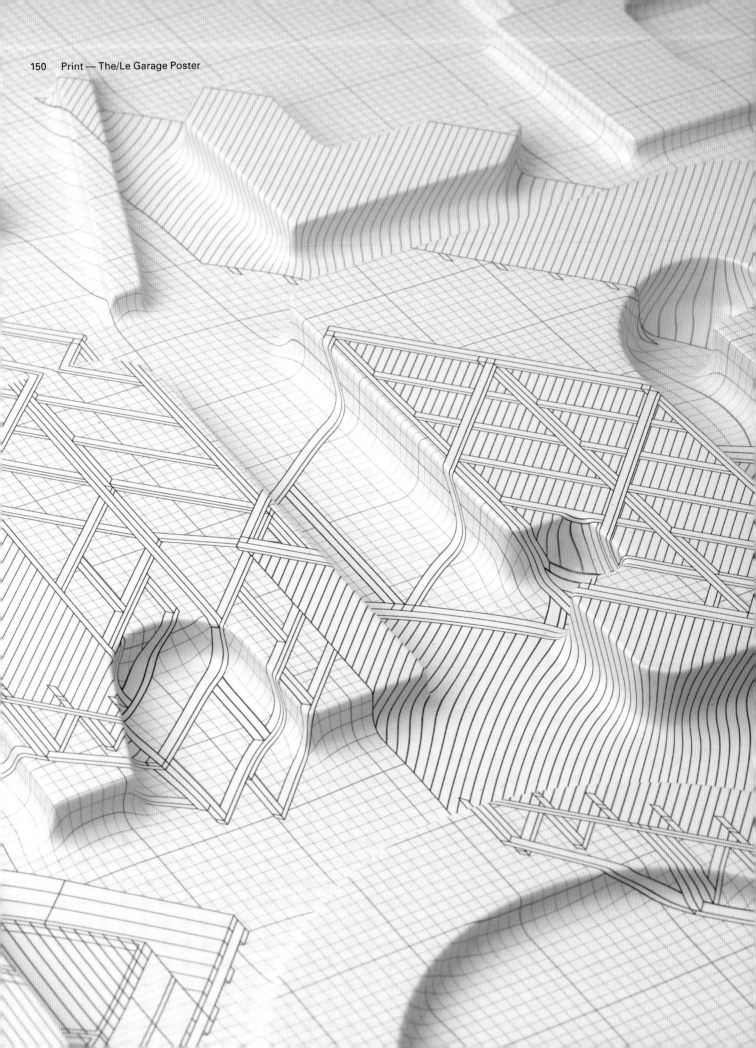

The/Le Garage
Paul Elliman/Graphic Thought Facility
15 éme Festival International de l'affiche et des arts graphiques
Chaumont (Haute—Marne): 15 mai au 27 juin 2004
The/Le Garage is commissioned by The British Council and Chaumont Poster Festival

Design: Paul Elliman/Graphic Thought Facility. Print: Plasticolor, Italy

Material
Rigid PVC

Process
Thermoforming

DEVIL'S ADVOCATE, DAVE CLARKE
TOM HINGSTON STUDIO

Tom Hingston Studio has worked with a wide range of fashion and music clients such as Mandarina Duck, Massive Attack and Gnarls Barkley. On this CD packaging for DJ Dave Clarke, thermoforming has been employed, but has been skewed to meet the demands of the opening and closing method, and to apply the logo. It is also the product of the consideration of a number of ideas and methods that have been filtered through the design process.

The project started with sourcing a collection of items—materials and process examples—that met the notion of something dark, scientific, Victorian and, at the same time, futuristic. The result also had to have some inbuilt sense of being degraded or having had a previous use. High-density foam could have provided a perfect solution to housing the CD itself, which would then be clad in some kind of print-treated board or plastic sleeve. However, it was found that black PVC or lower-grade thermoformable polypropylenes have a tendency to split and bubble when formed.

CDs are usually packed in an injection-moulded styrene hinged-lid box. The Dave Clarke CD had to be racked alongside these jewel cases at retail, and also had to have some kind of open and closing function that would fit with the thermoforming process. An integrated hinge could possibly have been the best solution, as it can be built into the tool at no extra expense. However, PVC materials can snap under the repeated stress this causes, so it was discounted. One further consideration in the development process was the fact that the lid and the base were two separate entities, one being degraded and the other perfect in finish—a marriage of two disparate components coming together as one entity.

Before further development of the packaging could take place, the text had to be tested to confirm that the dot-configuration font would form out of the material. Two things came to light—in thermoforming there is no capability of reading Mac files, and the conversion from Mac to PC turned some dots into ellipses that were not read, thus making for empty spaces on the logo. The second problem was that the dots were so small that the material was not being drawn into them when formed. The only (fairly drastic) solution was to drill right through the tool to make sure that all the text formed.

The final packaging consists of two elements: the base that houses the CD and the lid that slides over the top. The lid is a simple forming, with the flange that acts as a frame also serving as the runner for the sliding mechanism. This is very difficult to achieve as the material is heated for forming and has a tendency to cockle when bent, creating a wavy fold. At the foot of the lid is a stop that prevents the lid from sliding right through. The cutaway at the foot of the base makes it slide shut to create the rectangular shape. The centre boss has a slight undercut allowing the CD to lock in position. The tolerance on this element was very small, as the CD had to be able to be removed easily, and this was hampered by the material expanding and contracting at intervals throughout the production run.

If one compares *Devil's Advocate*'s dimensions to a conventional CD jewel case it is slightly taller to compensate for the mechanics of the packaging in addition to the size of a CD. This tends to be a common trait with unconventional CD packaging. In this instance, the end result proved highly successful, and was nominated for a D&AD award for music packaging.

Materials
Paper (Uncoated), Synthetic Paper

Processes
Embossing, Lithography

SKETCH LOOK BOOK
ICH & KAR

French designers Ich & Kar are Helena Ichbiah and Piotr Karczewski—they have worked for clients in the fields of music, fashion, food and architecture, including Givenchy, Yves Saint Laurent and Kiss Cool. In 2006, the pair were commissioned to design a look book for London restaurant and art space Sketch. The lavishly produced product was conceived as a brochure to be sent to carefully selected individuals around the world to promote Sketch's approach to the dining experience.

The visuals for the book are a series of unusual images of food that had been taken by photographer Erwan Frotin. The initial concept was that Frotin's photographs would be used for a series of posters, but the idea of this book evolved as a way of making a unified object out of the images.

The book is unusual in that it uses a synthetic paper, Polyart, for its text pages, chosen for its interesting feel. When creased, the pages turn well as a brochure at this dimension. It is also very light and not prone to finger marks. Given that the designers had used this particular type of paper before they had no concerns about printing with it. Cost, however, was a concern, but Polyart's ultimate suitability for the job of doing justice to Frotin's images quickly became apparent. As a foil to the inner pages, an uncoated paper was chosen for the book's outer slipcase, which was embossed with the title, further enhancing the highly tactile nature of the publication.

Confidence in using new substrates and proving their suitability by example can greatly assist in convincing a client that a method of manufacture will work. In the case of Sketch, the need to be innovative had already been established by the commissioning of Frotin's imagery and was expertly carried through by the designers in the choice of materials and production.

OFFERED TO YOU BY POMMERY

Materials
Silicone, Synthetic Paper

Processes
Lithography, Moulding, Screen Printing

ENEMY & LOVERS, SCRATCH MASSIVE
PIERRE-FRANÇOIS LETUÉ

Pierre-François 'PIF' Letué is a Paris-based designer and art director. His promotional packaging for Scratch Massive's much anticipated debut album *Enemy & Lovers* references his own previous packaging projects, in which access to the contents meant the destruction of packaging.

Letué formulated an idea around the most hi-tech reading possible of wrecking the packaging. The requirements of the project specified that the set had to contain an advance CD of the album, a page of printed biography and a promotional photograph. Combining the destructive aspects of previous works, and emulating the oppositional forces of the album's title, along with experiments he had made with silicone a few years previously, Letué adopted an idiosyncratic approach: in brief, a block of bathroom silicone moulded three times, the items placed inside it, then all sealed with another silicone block which had type moulded into it.

The experiment was a success, with the client's excited approval validating the production. The prototype was shown to a studio specializing in moulding for fashion and art projects. There was some reticence in producing the work but the supplier was intrigued to see the project develop. The only modification required was to print the literature on synthetic paper, as it is more stable than conventional paper and thus is better equipped to survive the immersion in silicone.

Reactions to the project are mixed. Some people frustrate themselves with the dilemma of whether to keep the packaging complete or destroy it, and opt for the former by preserving the object intact. Others embrace the project, destroying the cocoon-like packaging to get to the CD inside, sacrificing the object to the music. To satisfy the demands of both these parties, a second, increased production run was required.

Material
Wood

Process
Laser Etching

THE NORTH FACE: UNLIMITED
SATURDAY

Design agency Saturday has worked with international fashion and retail clients such as H&M, Kurt Geiger and Swarovski. In early 2006, they were approached by outdoor-clothing company The North Face to create packaging for a limited-edition CD to be sold in its stores.

The North Face specializes in high-fashion, high-performance outdoor wear —connecting with nature and being at one with the environment play a big part in the company's brand ethos. As an extension of this theme, The North Face Japan joined forces with the Gas Book series to embark on a series of limited-edition projects that started with the idea of 'Roots of Life'.

Saturday was invited to create the packaging for the third collaborative project —this mix CD compiled by Izumi/Minotaur. Continuing the theme of connecting with nature, two versions of the CD case were produced: a regular jewel case with printed-card slipcover, and a second limited-edition case made from real wood with a slide-out tray and intricate laser etching.

The design on the front cover of the wooden CD exactly mirrors the design on the card slipcover. Wood is not an obvious choice as CD packaging, but the laser-etched lines are extremely subtle on the wooden version and add texture to the otherwise smooth surface of the dark grain. The precision of the laser etching gives lines fine enough for the entire track listing to be included on the back of the case in the same size type as is used on the card version. And, even though the case is made from wood, the whole package is surprisingly light. 1000 copies of the limited-edition wooden CD case were released, with Gas Books handling the production in Japan.

The North Face Japan organized an exhibition of Saturday's work in one of their spaces to coincide with the launch. The CD went in-store in August 2006 and quickly sold out. Saturday's clever use of a low-tech, craft-based material in combination with a high-tech process gives an intriguing twist to a simple, everyday object.

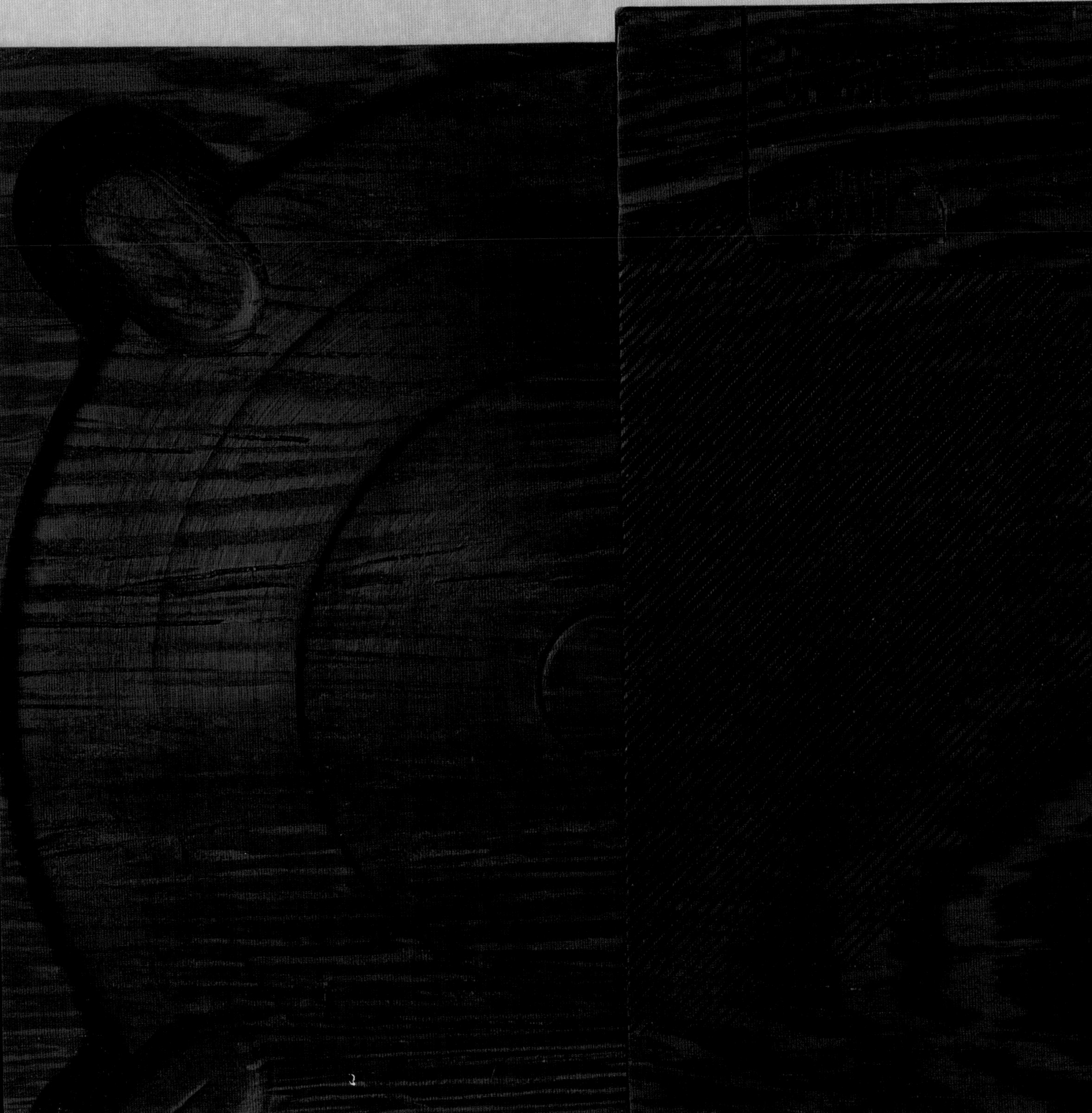

163

Ich&Kar Ich&Kar Ich&Kar
Pif Pif Pif Pif Pif Pif
SpMillot SpMillot SpMillot
Reclame Reclame Reclame

Materials
Grey Board, Paper (Uncoated)

Processes
Binding, Lithography

CONVERSATIONS VOLUME 1
ICH & KAR AND SPMILLOT

Conversations Volume 1 was designed by the French graphic-design duo Ich & Kar, in collaboration with French typographer SpMillot, and is described by its creators as a 108-page exhibition. Piles of these books were displayed in venues in London, Paris and Tokyo, and members of the public were allowed to take copies home.

The publication comprises a series of saddle-stitched booklets interspaced with panels of grey board cut away at the spine, thus emphasizing the space while also high-lighting the red, white and black staples. Closer inspection reveals the contributors' names repeat-printed on the spines of their respective booklets. The idea is that the book can be displayed as a free-standing object with its pages fanned out, and that the grey board represents the walls of an imaginary gallery.

This simple conceit was exceptionally time-consuming at the finishing stage, with the person gluing the books together spending five weeks working on it solidly. The project had previously been proposed to a number of finishers who refused to put it together. This highlights a problem with complicated projects. What looks simple as a paper dummy in the studio is often not suitable, or considered, for manufacture in large volumes. This serves to stress just how important early conversations with suppliers are in ensuring that a project is completed without any hitches or compromises, and that an end result is reached that is to everyone's satisfaction. Finishing problems aside, *Conversations Volume 1* has now become highly sought after.

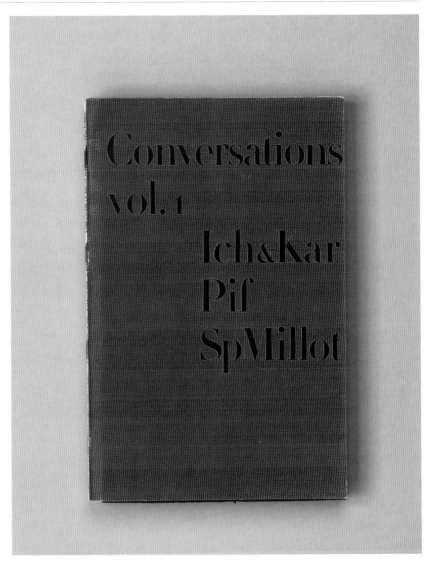

Material
Paper (Uncoated)

Processes
Binding, Hand Folding, Lithography

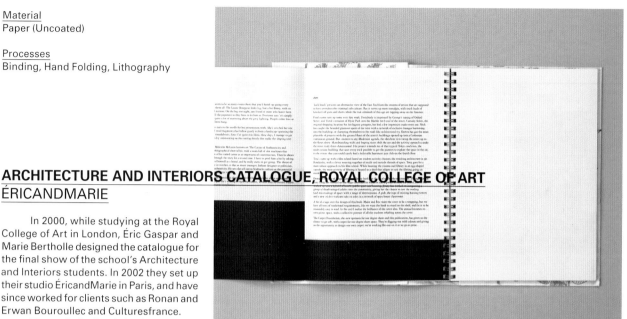

ARCHITECTURE AND INTERIORS CATALOGUE, ROYAL COLLEGE OF ART
ÉRICANDMARIE

In 2000, while studying at the Royal College of Art in London, Éric Gaspar and Marie Bertholle designed the catalogue for the final show of the school's Architecture and Interiors students. In 2002 they set up their studio ÉricandMarie in Paris, and have since worked for clients such as Ronan and Erwan Bouroullec and Culturesfrance.

The main body of the Architecture and Interiors catalogue consists of pages wire bound with a steel wire. Meanwhile, a more complex configuration of folded paper wrapped around the outside of the book acts as a dust jacket. This folds out to a double-sided poster showing on one side a pattern made up of full-length photographs of all the students, while the other side is decorated with a leaf motif. Three vertical folds and five horizontal folds are used to transform the unfurled poster into a dust jacket, so that sections of both the front and back of the poster are visible as layers on the covers of the book.

The folding process was too complex to be done mechanically, so each of the 2000 copies of the catalogue was folded by hand. The main problem encountered by the designers was how to affix the poster to the main body of the book. Eventually this was done by binding a small cardboard panel to the back of the book and gluing this to a section of the poster.

Hand finishing will occasionally be the only resolution that will produce the desired result for a project. It can be time-consuming if undertaken by yourself, and also hamper work on other projects—as with most processes there are a number of specialized companies that undertake this type of work. It is quite normal for such companies to take on complicated folding and creasing projects, sometimes with very high numbers of items. It is important to determine how you wish this aspect of the project to work, as last-minute changes to instructions or to the stocks can have a detrimental effect on cost.

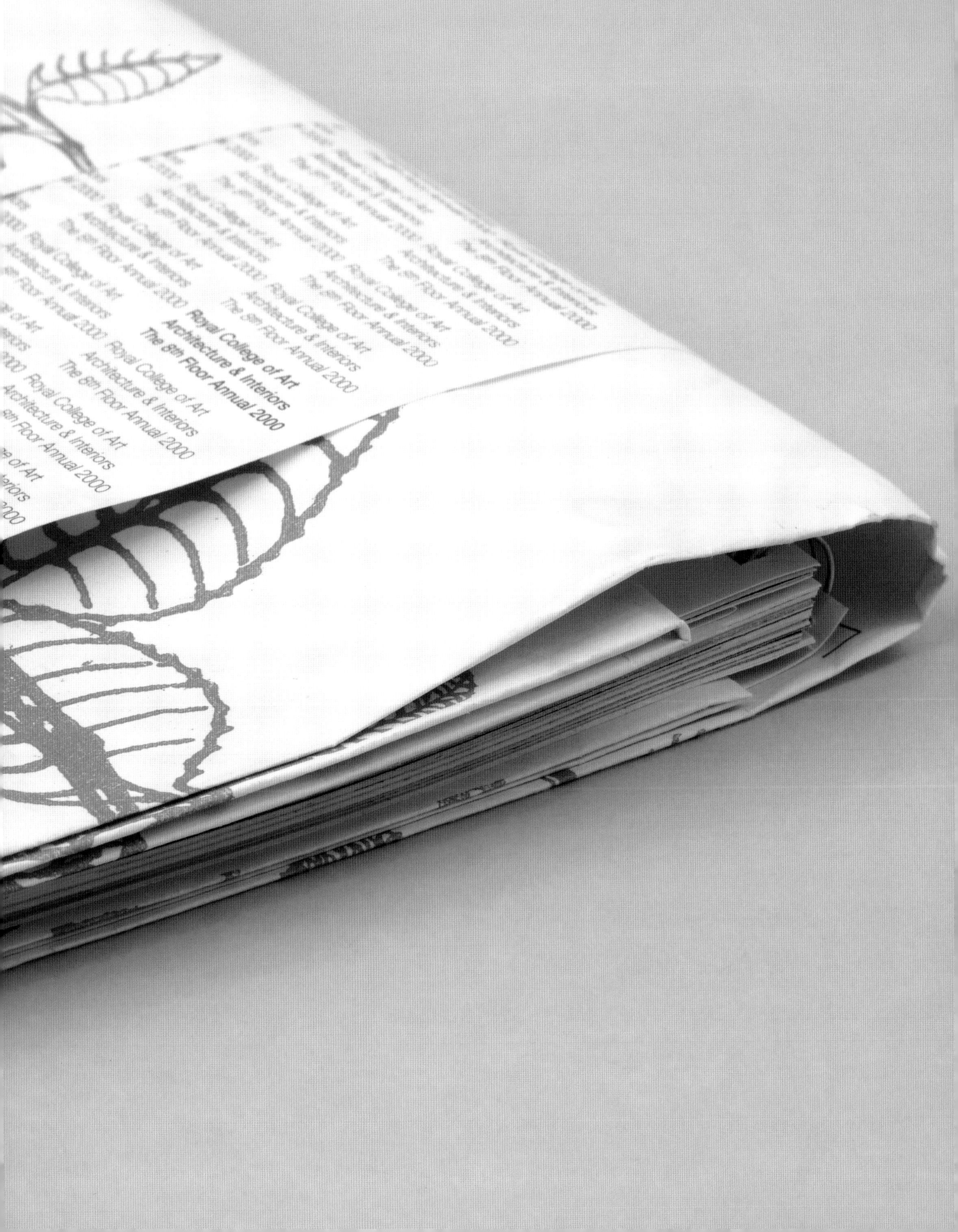

Royal College of Art
Architecture & Interiors
The 6th Floor Annual 2000

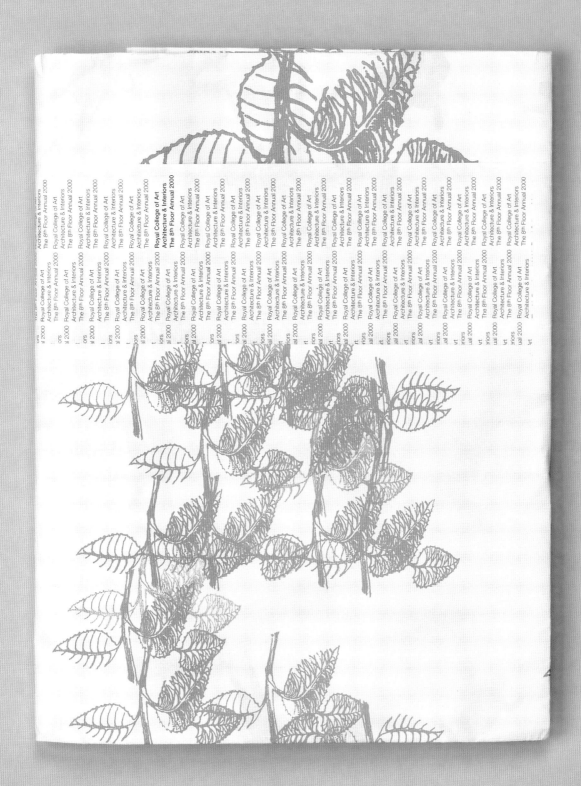

ADI
RIO

Fórum
Laus 05

PURA
SEDA
MGZ

Una revista multilingüe
con 9 conferencias, 7 workshops,
una fiesta y un montón de fotos
de una mona vestida de seda.

Que
Se Muera
Lo Feo

Materials
Newsprint, Paper (Folding Boxboard;
Uncoated), Rubber Bands

Processes
Binding, Embossing, Lithography, Rotary
Printing

PURA SEDA MAGAZINE
ALBERT FOLCH STUDIO

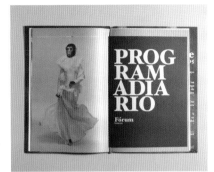

Albert Folch Studio (AFS) is a Barce-
lona-based agency. Working alongside Omar
Sosa, Albert Folch creates mainly print-based
projects for fashion brands and magazines,
as well as art catalogues. They also undertake
collaborations with visual artists.

Pura Seda Magazine was produced
as the programme of activities for Laus 05
(an annual graphic design and visual com-
munication awards scheme and conference
organized by the Spanish design association
AGD-FAD). 'Pura Seda' translates as 'pure
silk'—the campaign for the conference was
based on the phrase *'Aunque la mona se
vista de seda, mona se queda'* (roughly trans-
lated, this means 'You can dress a monkey
in silk, but it will still be a monkey'). Hence
the cover of *Pura Seda Magazine* sports a
lady chimp in a silk outfit, one of many that
appear throughout the brochure. Folch had
originally wanted a typographic cover but
the client wanted to go down the simian
route. The *Pura Seda* logo was also embossed
on the cover.

The publication uses a rough news-
print-type paper for its 56 text pages, with
a slightly larger heavy boxboard cover that
protects the contents. There is a smaller
one-colour, four-page section in the middle
that summarizes all the workshops, talks
and other activities. A long rubber band
holds everything together, taking the place
of the more traditional method of saddle
stitching. This band had to be specifically
selected for its elasticity and diameter to
ensure that it did not damage the cover and
pages when wrapped around them.

Folch used the rotary printing method
commonly employed to print newspapers
for the bulk of the piece—this was partly
because of budgetary restrictions and partly because of the tight deadlines which he
had to work to. Folch had no experience of
rotary printing and had to adapt his design
to fit within the demands of the process,
particularly the resolution and settings of
the colour images. A great deal of coordina-
tion was needed with a second printing
company that was handling both the cover
and the middle section using the more conventional litho method. The contrast in the
quality of the two printing methods is very
obvious, since the same image is repeated

on the first page of the text section as on
the cover.

Folch's ingenious use of materials
gives a suitably exciting and vibrant feel to
the brochure, turning what would usually
be a disposable magazine into an item that
attendees would want to keep and refer to
long after the conference was over.

Materials
Paper (Board; Uncoated)

Processes
Binding, Die Cutting, Screen Printing

SPACE CAKE, CHANEL HAUTE COUTURE DVD
PIERRE-FRANÇOIS LETUÉ

Each Chanel fashion show is filmed and a DVD produced that is sent to all of Chanel's boutiques around the world. They are also distributed to privileged customers and members of the press. Several movies are created showing different facets of each collection, including the runway show, the details of garments and an edit of the show plus interviews.

The need for exclusive packaging to accompany each new show has been emphasized by the art director Pierre-François Letué. The sets for these shows are as unique as the catalogues that come after, and he felt that, given the nature of the event, it was appropriate to create something that would become a highly covetable piece.

Using a stage set that was modelled on a wedding cake as the loose basis for the idea, along with the Letué's own references and inspiration, the packaging for the DVD took shape. He had always harboured a desire to produce a children's board book, and the DVD packaging reflects this: made from four thick pages, it is bound on one side with white tape. To achieve the required finish, a higher quality of paper had to be mounted to a thicker, creamier coloured board—the client insisted on a higher quality finish than the original prototype in return for a tripling of the production costs. The pages reveal four die-cut concentric circles, with a hole in the back cover—these mirror the tiers of a wedding cake, and the intertwined letters of the Chanel logo.

The matt-black DVD is screen printed with a black gloss ink, which produces a subtle effect. The disc is then mounted into a recess in the front cover, and the black die-cut, loose-leaf card is slipped in. This was made from a substrate that is supplied with a smooth rubberized coating, giving a stark contrast to the roughness of the white uncoated stock. A light cardboard slipcase is employed so that the type of DVD can be indicated on the cover.

● PAL

○ NTSC

○ SHOW ONLY

○ M.OFF

● M.OR

Some problems were encountered with the alignment and complicated die cutting of the pages. Also, the supplier in charge of printing the DVD disc could not understand the desired effect of the black-on-black print at first. Despite this, Letué has created an intriguing and tactile object befitting such a prestigious client.

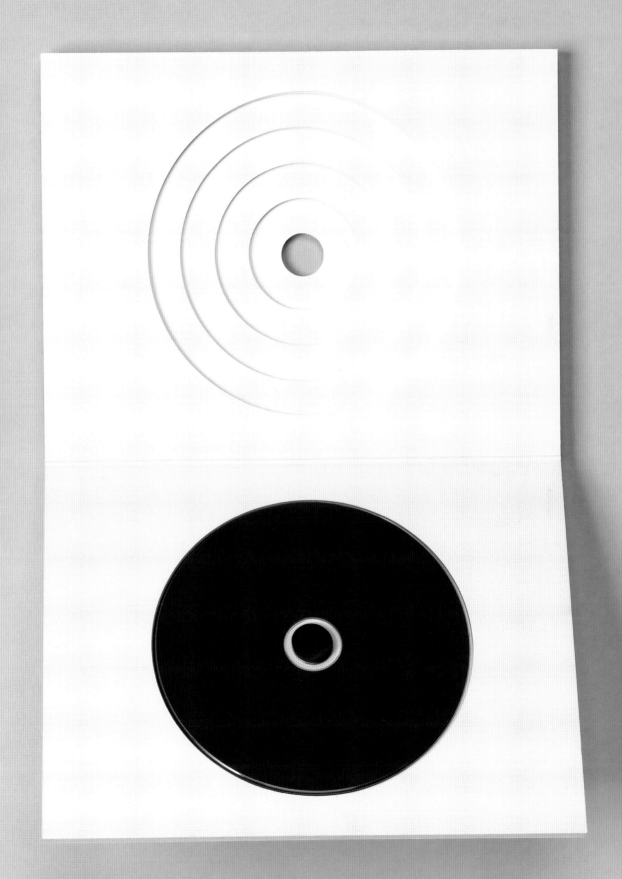

Materials
Coloured Paper, Paper (Uncoated; Card)

Processes
Binding, Lithography, Rigid Box Making

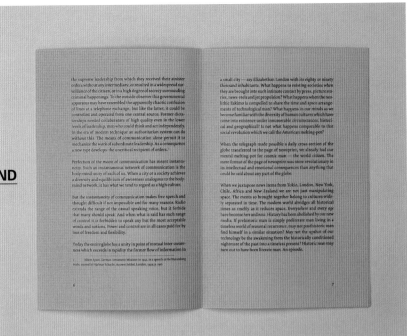

MARSHALL MCLUHAN UNBOUND
ONLAB

Marshall McLuhan Unbound was conceived as an intriguing and manageable way of presenting the ideas of the legendary Canadian educator and theorist Marshall McLuhan. Credited with coining phrases such as 'the global village' and 'the medium is the message', McLuhan's often complex texts are still considered to be essential reading matter for anyone studying media or communications.

Based in Berlin, onlab participates in both collaborative and self-initiated projects, and co-founded etc. publications, a Berlin-based forum for independent publishing. They were commissioned to design this boxed set of McLuhan's essays by Robert Klanten of design publisher and consultancy Die Gestalten Verlag. The collection of 20 individual booklets comprises 19 of McLuhan's essays plus an introductory text by W. Terrence Gordon, and was published in an edition of 4000 copies.

While the processes involved (four-colour lithography and stapling) in *Marshall McLuhan Unbound* may not be particularly specialized, the concept itself was difficult to achieve and extra time was needed by the designers to run preliminary tests with the finishing. The real key to the successful execution of this project was complete accuracy in the binding and finishing stages.

The striking slipcase features bold italicized typography and a design comprising of overlaid multicoloured concentric rings. This same graphic language is also used on the 20 booklets, each of which has a different cover—the concentric rings gradually come together until they make a complete circle on the last essay, mirroring the reader's growing understanding of the subject matter as they progress through the series. The open end of the slipcase is cut at opposite acute angles on each side —while this may seem at first to be mere styling, it is actually a very practical device that allows the reader easy access to the booklets from each side of the slipcase.

Although the booklets have been stapled and therefore do not have a spine, a four-millimetre area has been overprinted on each, which creates the effect of a spine, so that when all the volumes are placed in order inside the case, the word 'Unbound'

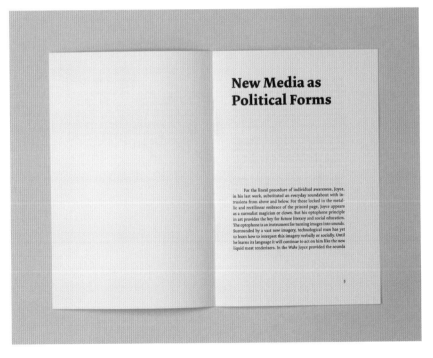

is spelled out. The effect is dramatic—the intelligent graphic devices and ingenious finishing throughout the project turn what might have been a very dry textbook into an extremely covetable object.

Materials
Coloured Paper, Paper
(Coated; Uncoated)

Processes
Binding, Lithography

THE ONE WEEKEND BOOK SERIES: GRAPHIC TOURISM SINCE 2003
TWOPOINTS.NET

Small but internationally active studio TwoPoints.net is run out of Barcelona by Martin Laurenz, working for cultural and music clients including publishing house Eichborn, Volkswagen's Hotel Fox and bands such as Cultured Pearls and Kay Cee. Laurenz is also author of a unique publishing project entitled *The One Weekend Book Series* that he initiated in 2003 while living in Frankfurt Am Main in Germany. The project has seen Laurenz pair up with other designers and collaborators over a series of weekends in different cities in order to produce a written and visual memento of their experiences as 'graphic tourists'.

The project was borne out of Laurenz's desire to create work outside his commercial practice. With each of his guest artists he made and published a 48-page book based on experiences over single weekends in Frankfurt Am Main, Copenhagen, Berlin and New York. At first these booklets were distributed individually in a handful of select European bookshops, but in 2006 they were also published as a collection by Actar. The approach to the production of this collection was informed by Laurenz's desire to create a cohesive whole but also maintain a sense of the books as individual works and stay true to the project's original spirit. 'We used all kinds of materials, everything we found and everything that was available to glue on to a piece of paper,' says Laurenz of the production of the original books. 'We were just hungry to experiment with unusual materials as the computer was a forbidden tool.' From the material gathered, the designers produced collages, illustrations and texts, which were photocopied, stapled and numbered by hand.

In the final collected volume, various coloured paper stocks are employed to differentiate the five original books. This colour-coding device is further reinforced by binding the sections with an exposed spine, which leaves these colours visible. The volume is housed within a jacket with a unique folding system comprising five panels and a spine section, which was developed especially for *The One Weekend Book Series*. In addition, a further 36-page black-and-white introductory section is stapled within the cover.

The folder-like cover was Laurenz's solution to a production problem that arose from his original design concept, which was simply to stitch the whole book together. This proved unworkable, as the binding was not strong enough for the number of pages to be held together. Laurenz decided to separate the introductory section and attach it to its own cover-cum-folder, allowing the rest of the inner sections to function as an autonomous, removable whole. 'I loved the solution,' he says, 'because the production underlines the difference between both parts ... and makes it easier to cross-reference the commentary in the introduction with the illustrations in the five books.'

The result is a triumph of unusual book publishing. 'I wanted to create a book for book lovers,' explains Laurenz, 'a book that someone would like to look at while sitting at home with a cup of tea.'

The One Weekend
Book Series

Volume One / July 2003
Friendship and Guilt

by M. Leamer & T. Woodenstein

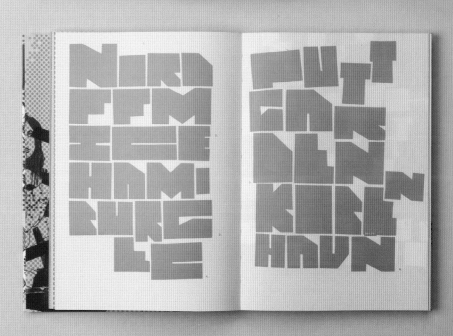

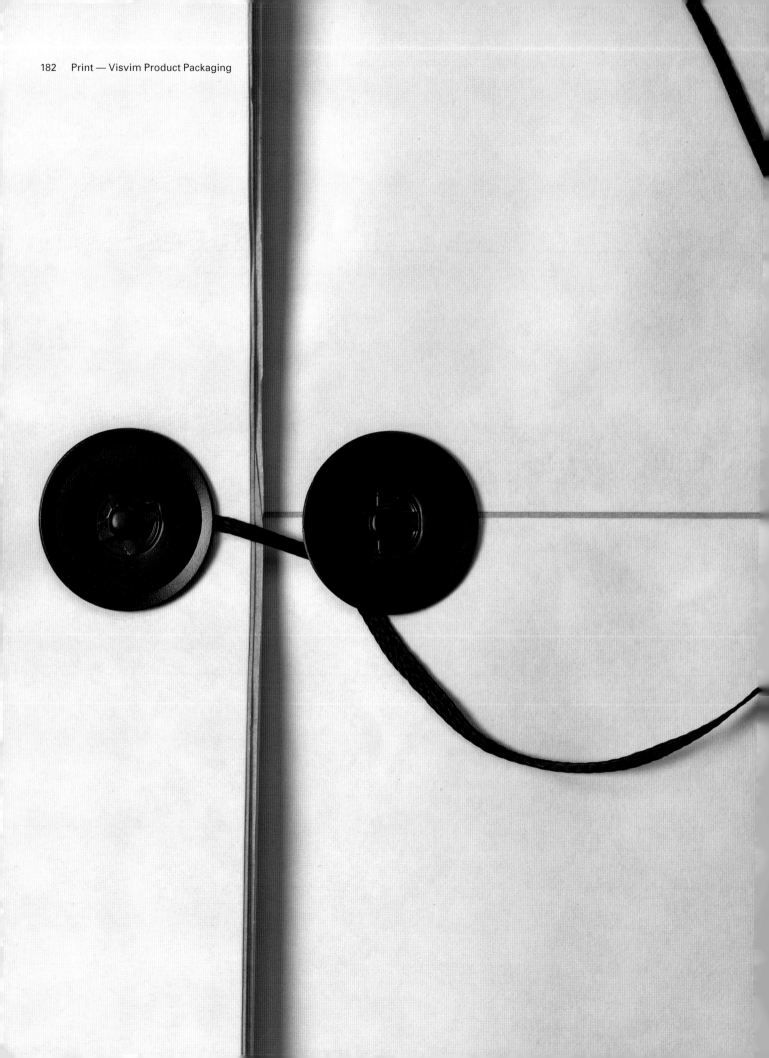

visvim.

visvim.

Materials
Corrugated Cardboard, Paper (Recycled),
Tyvek

Processes
Carton Making, Closures, Die Cutting,
Hand Finishing, Lithography, Screen
Printing

VISVIM PRODUCT PACKAGING
CUBISM INC.

Visvim/CUBISM inc. is a footwear and
apparel company producing a range of shoes
and clothing with an unparalleled focus on
both materials and finishing under creative
director Hiroki Nakamura. This attention to
detail is transferred to its packaging.

Their packaging is influenced by traditional Japanese stationery, but also by
items that function outside their original
intended use. At the core of the company's
ethos for its products is a desire for them
to be used. The packaging had to relay this
message at a very basic level, while not
becoming a distraction. It is white with a
contrasting black disc-and-string closure
—the whole is engineered for reuse once
the original item has been removed.

The original concept was to remove
any sort of gimmickry from the packaging,
resulting in something clean, simple and
organic, and complementary to the product
itself, with little or no branding at all. The
packaging is intended to hold no influence
over perceptions of the product, but rather
create a sense of negative space for the
exhibition of the product, much like a gallery
exhibits a work of art.

The manufacturing methods used for
these projects are not regarded as unconventional, but rely heavily on hand finishing.
Visvim wanted their footwear, candle and
tissue boxes to have a purpose outside of
simply holding a product, so the designers
endeavoured to keep the quality as high as
possible to encourage their reuse over an
extended time period. Because of their sizes,
the bags for the company's underwear were
hand cut and assembled. The black discs
used with the strings for closure also had
to be a special size and, because of this, a
manufacturer had to be found to assemble
this element by hand.

Packaging is extremely important to
the company, but it is the product that is
being sold, not its wrapping. Through their
attention to detail, Visvim wished to com-
municate to customers that they had shown
a similar degree of care and craft in their
approach to the object within.

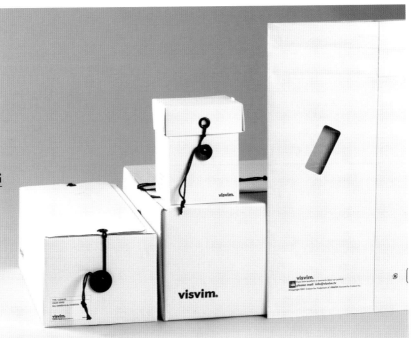

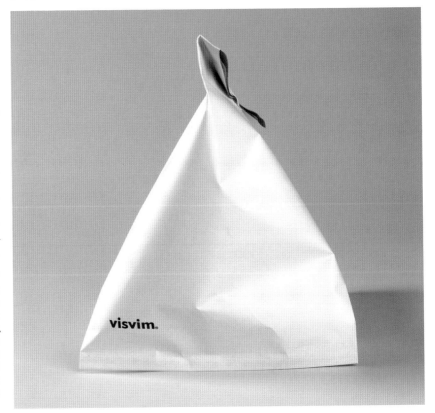

Material
Paper (Card)

Processes
Die Cutting, Lithography

HOTEL EXHIBITION CARDS
PAUL HETHERINGTON

British graphic designer and art director Paul Hetherington is creative director
of online art and fashion enterprise SHOW-
studio. He is also creative director for east
London art space Hotel, and created the
gallery's visual identity and a standardized
system of promotional cards and invitations
for exhibitions.

While the size and shape of the cards
change from show to show, one constant
feature is their radius corners. Hetherington
knew from previous experience that corners
could be rounded off using a simple tool
that acts as a rudimentary cutter, which is
applied after guillotining. Although this process lacked the precision of die-cut finishing,
it was only a fraction of the cost.

This feature of the identity was conceived as one part of a wider set of visual
devices that together reflects the atmosphere
and ethos of Hotel. The gallery is run by
Darren Flook and Cristabel Stewart from
their home on Bethnal Green Road, London.
Artists from outside London are invited to
stay for the duration of their exhibition and
participate in events and talks around the
show. The pair's home-cum-gallery is situ-
ated in a small, late-nineteenth-century ter-
race, and the visual identity is designed to
reflect this stark, Dickensian environment.
The invitation format was inspired by paper
place settings at the Quality Chop House
in London—a traditional Victorian diner in
Farringdon, where simple white sheets with
rounded corners are used as settings.

The uncomplicated, understated invites are printed in single colours on a
coated board, and are purely typographic,
using a basic layout with the text centralized.
The main feature is the artist's name, the
length of which dictates the card's size and
shape. This creates variety in an otherwise
regularized format and, says Hetherington,
'is intended to quickly create a history and
give the impression of "change over time",
like a mismatched set of hotel crockery
acquired over time.' By means of a simple
print-finishing device, Hetherington has
summoned up the setting, atmosphere and
character of the Hotel gallery.

HTTP://WWW.GENERALHOTEL.ORG

_Alastair
MacKinven_

JERKIN' Off THE ... THE CAT

PP...

...PM

HTTP://WWW.GENERALHOTEL.ORG

...GENERALHOTEL.ORG

...PPOINTMENT
...GREEN

Steven

HTTP://WWW.GENERALHOTEL.

...rite Teplin_

...R ARMOUR A
...VIEW SATURDAY 14TH MAY 6–9PM

Martin

...RY ¶ 9TH OCT–7TH NOV 2004
... FRIDAY 8TH OCT 6–9PM

...TEL

...E2 6QA TEL +44 (0)20 7729 3122 INFO@GENERALHOTEL.ORG

HOTEL
...EN ROAD, LONDON E2 6QA TEL +44 (0)20 7729 3122 INFO@GENERALHOTEL.ORG

HTTP://WWW.GENERALHOTEL.ORG

HTTP://WWW.GENERALHOTEL.ORG

...nael
...er_

...G WHORE"
...EW FRIDAY 24TH FEB 6–9PM

...avid
...onan_

OPEN: THUR–SUN 12–6PM OR BY APPOINTMENT
UNDERGROUND – BETHNAL GREEN

HTTP://WWW.GENERALHOTEL.ORG

David Noonan

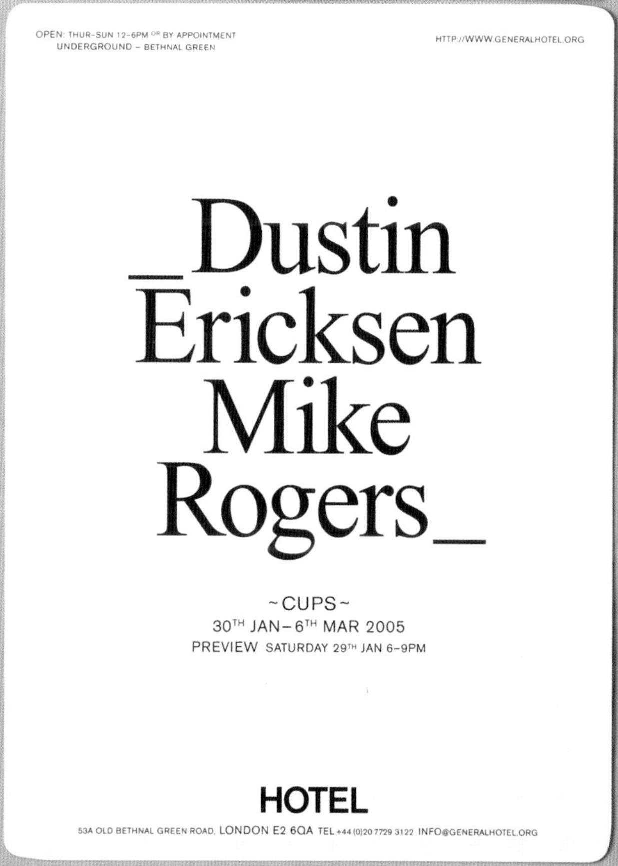

~~~FIELDS~~~

16TH OCT–20TH NOV 2005   PREVIEW SATURDAY 15TH OCT 6–9PM

HOTEL

53 OLD BETHNAL GREEN ROAD. LONDON E2 6QA TEL +44 (0)20 7729 3122 INFO@GENERALHOTEL.ORG

OPEN: THUR–SUN 12–6PM OR BY APPOINTMENT
UNDERGROUND – BETHNAL GREEN

HTTP://WWW.GENERALHOTEL.ORG

Carter

11TH DEC 2005–4TH FEB 2006
PREVIEW SATURDAY 10TH DEC 6–9PM

HOTEL

53 OLD BETHNAL GREEN ROAD. LONDON E2 6QA TEL +44 (0)20 7729 3122 INFO@GENERALHOTEL.ORG

OPEN: THUR–SUN 12–6PM OR BY APPOINTMENT
UNDERGROUND – BETHNAL GREEN

HTTP://WWW.GENERALHOTEL.ORG

Alastair MacKinven

JERKIN' Off THE DOG TO FEED THE CAT

14TH APR–29TH MAY 2006
PREVIEW THURSDAY 13TH APR 6–9PM

HOTEL

53 OLD BETHNAL GREEN ROAD. LONDON E2 6QA TEL +44 (0)20 7729 3122 INFO@GENERALHOTEL.ORG

OPEN: THUR–SUN 12–6PM OR BY APPOINTMENT
UNDERGROUND – BETHNAL GREEN

HTTP://WWW.GENERALHOTEL.ORG

Dustin Ericksen Mike Rogers

~CUPS~

30TH JAN–6TH MAR 2005
PREVIEW SATURDAY 29TH JAN 6–9PM

HOTEL

53A OLD BETHNAL GREEN ROAD. LONDON E2 6QA TEL +44 (0)20 7729 3122 INFO@GENERALHOTEL.ORG

OPEN: THUR–SUN 12–6PM OR BY APPOINTMENT
UNDERGROUND – BETHNAL GREEN

HTTP://WWW.GENERALHOTEL.ORG

Daria Martin

CLO§EUP GALLERY ¶ 9TH OCT–7TH NOV 2004
PREVIEW FRIDAY 8TH OCT 6–9PM

HOTEL

53A OLD BETHNAL GREEN ROAD. LONDON E2 6QA TEL +44 (0)20 7729 3122 INFO@GENERALHOTEL.ORG

CD6
K Greatest
as chosen by Bjork   hits

[16] Fernando

[24] Melancholy

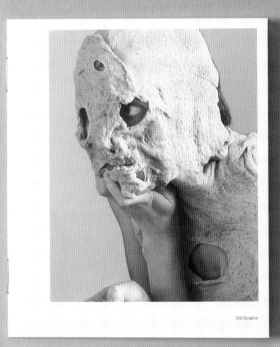

[26] Sculptor

Materials
Flexible PVC, Paper (Coated; Uncoated),
Polypropylene

Processes
Binding, Closures, Embossing,
HF Welding, Injection Moulding,
Lithography

FAMILY TREE: A TAXONOMY OF SONG, BJÖRK
M/M (PARIS)

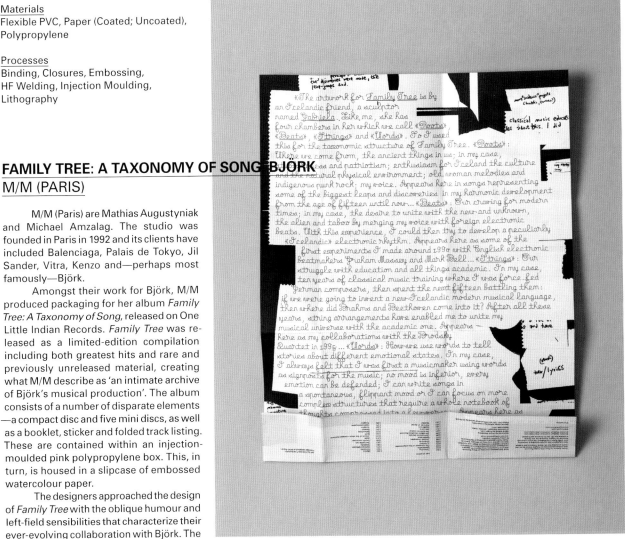

M/M (Paris) are Mathias Augustyniak
and Michael Amzalag. The studio was
founded in Paris in 1992 and its clients have
included Balenciaga, Palais de Tokyo, Jil
Sander, Vitra, Kenzo and—perhaps most
famously—Björk.

Amongst their work for Björk, M/M
produced packaging for her album *Family
Tree: A Taxonomy of Song*, released on One
Little Indian Records. *Family Tree* was released as a limited-edition compilation
including both greatest hits and rare and
previously unreleased material, creating
what M/M describe as 'an intimate archive
of Björk's musical production'. The album
consists of a number of disparate elements
—a compact disc and five mini discs, as well
as a booklet, sticker and folded track listing.
These are contained within an injection-
moulded pink polypropylene box. This, in
turn, is housed in a slipcase of embossed
watercolour paper.

The designers approached the design
of *Family Tree* with the oblique humour and
left-field sensibilities that characterize their
ever-evolving collaboration with Björk. The
choice of materials, together with the art
direction in *Family Tree*, are part of a narrative constructed around the whole project.
The watercolour paper and polypropylene
of the cover were chosen for their contrasting textures and to create a relationship
between organic and industrial processes.
The plastic box was especially designed for
the project, and M/M had not used either
material before to aid them in development
of the project: 'We wanted the packaging
to look like a CD box as seen through the
eyes of an alien … Inside the box is a picture
of a living creature with a pink nose and a
white plaster body, who is manufacturing
the box set.'

Despite the fact that each one of the
elements within this box set is a record-
industry standard, the way that they have
been assembled is highly original. M/M did
encounter a few problems as a result of this
idiosyncratic approach. The total thickness
of all the objects was underestimated, which
made closing the single fastener on the box
problematic, so it could have benefited from
a second fastener. Despite this, the finished
item is a success. 'The delicate clumsiness

of the whole object,' say M/M, 'has its own
charm. It looks alive, as if it is breathing,
which is great as objects never breathe.'
The endorsement for its innovation was a
nomination for best packaging at the 2004
Grammy Awards.

Material
Paper (Folding Boxboard)

Processes
Foil Blocking, Inks (Scented), Lithography,
Screen Printing

SCRATCH AND SNIFF EP, FUTURE LOOP FOUNDATION
BIG ACTIVE

Big Active is a London-based creative consultancy specializing in art direction, graphic design and the management of a select group of illustrators and photographers. They were commissioned to design a record sleeve for Future Loop Foundation's *Scratch and Sniff* EP, a limited-edition, vinyl-only release that was born as much out of a desire to create an interesting sleeve as by the music itself.

Very much a collaboration between the designers and Future Loop Foundation, Big Active were approached in the early stages of the project, when a working theme of 'summertime' had been established but no other titles were decided. *Scratch and Sniff*, then, was a title born out of the unusual production process that the designers employed for the sleeve. Taking inspiration from the summer theme, Big Active wanted to accentuate ideas associated with the season, such as colour and stimulation of the senses.

The sleeve was printed as a limited edition of 1000 copies, featuring illustrations by Big Active artist Jasper Goodall. Bubble gum, ice cream, bike riding and cloudless skies help capture an innocent, ideal vision of summer. 'The overall mood we aimed to evoke,' says Big Active creative director Gerard Saint, 'was one of childhood memories.' The vibrant print effect was achieved by replacing the cyan, magenta and yellow with bright day-glo colours to maximize the fluorescent appearance of the illustrations, which also helped to ensure that print costs did not escalate. Saint continues, 'The inner bag's text is printed white out of fluorescent yellow, which makes the typography so bright and dazzling it is almost impossible to read—an effect not dissimilar to staring into the sun.'

The application of scented inks further intensifies the visceral experience of these interactive sleeves. This ink is water-based and will not, therefore, adhere to print that has been varnished, but will scratch off. Therefore it has to be screen printed on unvarnished print, which can mark and scuff. In this instance, it did not pose a significant problem as the colours were not dark in tone. Scented ink does, however, have a tendency to lose its potency over time. This seems to be peculiar to certain fragrances —the grass scent on this sleeve has become increasingly cologne-like over time.

193

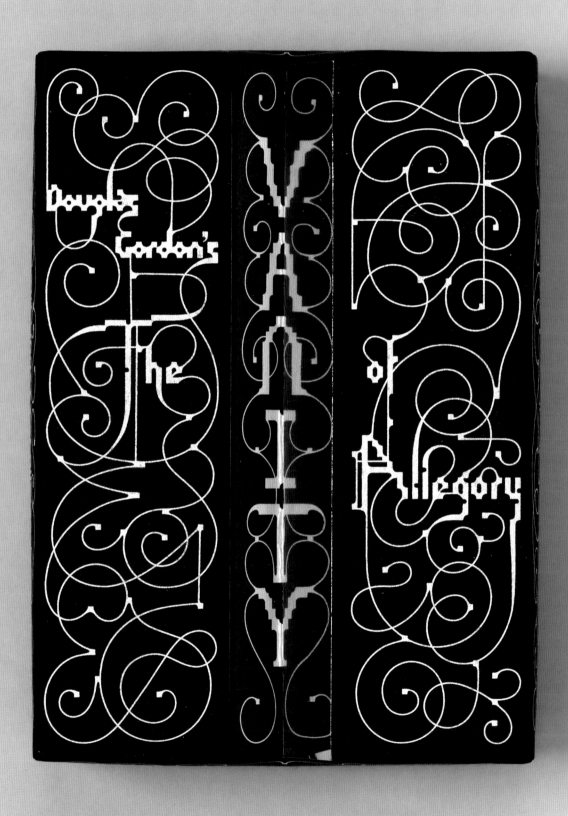

Materials
Mirri-Board, Paper (Card; Coated)

Processes
Carton Making, Die Cutting,
Hand Finishing, Lithography

THE VANITY OF ALLEGORY CATALOGUE
SAGMEISTER INC.

New York-based Sagmeister Inc., founded in 1993 and headed by Stefan Sagmeister, is a studio renowned for its innovative, uncompromising work for clients that range from TimeWarner to the Rolling Stones. In this catalogue for artist Douglas Gordon's 2005 show, *The Vanity of Allegory*, at the Berlin Guggenheim, Sagmeister and designer Matthias Ernstberger created a portable version of the entire exhibition by reproducing each of the works as postcards housed in a box.

The exhibition comprised a diverse range of work by artists (including Man Ray, Matthew Barney and Gordon himself), film footage (from Disney to the films of Kenneth Anger) and portrait photography (of subjects including Joseph Beuys and Leigh Bowery). This was effectively a form of self-portraiture in the guise of a group exhibition, through which Gordon explored ideas of self-depiction and the storytelling possibilities of self-portraiture. Sagmeister replicated the ideas about collecting explored in the show in his approach to the catalogue. Instead of a traditional bound book, this catalogue is a mutable collection of images, open to further interpretation and change at the hands of the viewer/reader.

The complex production of the box housing the cards further embodies Gordon's ideas. Reflection—specifically as a way of elucidating meaning—is used here literally, with a vertically positioned mirrored strip completing, when the box is tilted, the right-hand side of the letters V, A, N, I, T, Y. The mirror plate sits on one plane of an indented V-shaped trough that was created using folding. The rest of the black box is decorated with ornate type by Marion Bantjes.

An early design for the catalogue involved a much more complex mirror, which Sagmeister describes as 'pyramidical and gorgeous but quite intrusive to the work of the artist'. For the design that finally went into production they had also considered a paper-over-board construction, but eliminated it for budgetary reasons. Sagmeister also reveals that, with hindsight, he would have chosen a rigid box construction in order to better support the weight of the contents. Despite this, the final product is a successful and unusual catalogue that provides a lasting memento of the ideas explored in Gordon's exhibition.

<u>Materials</u>
Paper (Uncoated), Polythene,
Self-Adhesive

<u>Processes</u>
Hand Finishing, Photocopying

FAMOUS ISSUE 6, 'UNOFFICIAL IDENTITIES'
<u>EVENT10 AND TSUNAMI-ADDICTION</u>

Event10 is artist and graphic design-er Benoit Robert. He works on the visual identities of brands; on projects in music, fashion and art; and for cultural institutions. *Famous* magazine was started in 2002 as a fanzine to promote experimental music label Tsunami-Addiction. The project is still co-ordinated by label head Reiko Underwater. Just 250 copies of the first issues were printed, along with 20 copies of the accom-panying poster. The original concept for the magazine was to produce an entirely white magazine, with no visuals, just the names of real or virtual 'anti-contributors'. This idea was dropped in favour of a more diverse approach, looking at a different theme each month.

Famous aims to be theoretical and practical, intimate and mundane. The theme and format change every time; sometimes the magazine is screen printed, or soaked in water (as with issue 4), or in red ink (as with issue 6, featured here). The limited number of copies produced means that the magazine is manufactured by hand, giving it the feel of an art piece. For issue 6, the chosen theme was 'Unofficial Identities'. The magazine is simply stapled together, and consists of A4 black-and-white photo-copied sheets. This printing method was employed for financial reasons, but it also reinforces the subversive, quasi-political pamphlet feel and contents—the image on the cover is drawn from a feature about politically active New York youths entitled 'NYC Undercovered Anarkids'.

A dramatic stripe of bright red, which has been blotted along the spine and through the centre spread, gives a random effect to each copy, while also providing a stark contrast to the intense black used through-out the issue. This feature is carried through onto the packaging in which the magazine is distributed—a clear self-adhesive-backed document wallet, as seen in stationery cata-logues. This is regarded by Event10 as a fragile, inconvenient form of packaging, as the backing paper is soft and has a tendency to come off in transit or when being screen printed, for example.

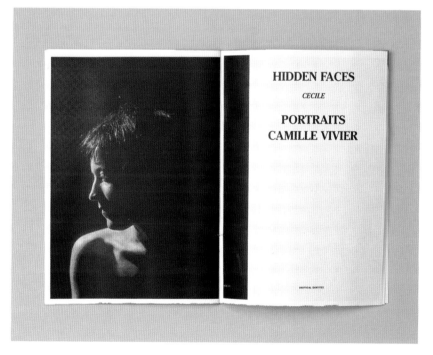

Famous magazine is now published quarterly, is distributed and sold in book-stores, and has a print run of 1000, but each issue remains experimental and unique, with materials and processes selected for their relevance to the theme.

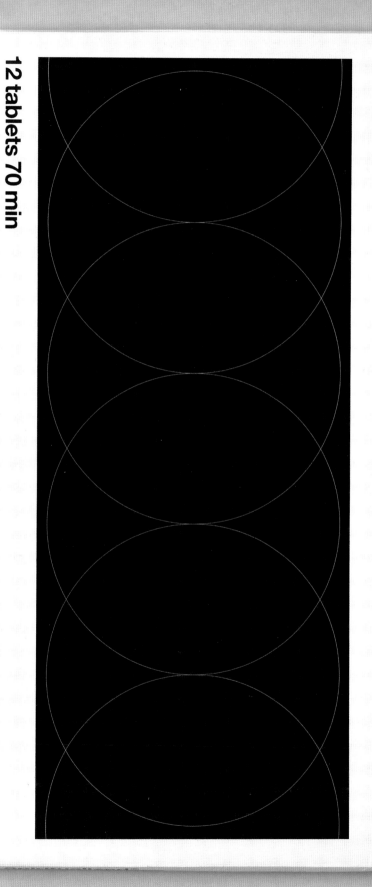

Spiritualized®

Ladies and gentlemen we are floating in space   B P

12 tablets 70 min

Materials
Foil, Paper (Folding Boxboard; Uncoated),
Rigid PVC, Self-Adhesive

Processes
Carton Making, Lithography,
Thermoforming

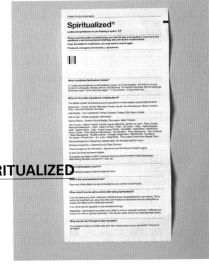

LADIES AND GENTLEMEN WE ARE FLOATING IN SPACE, SPIRITUALIZED
FARROW DESIGN/SPACEMAN

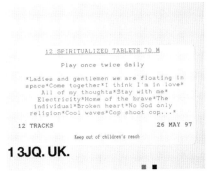

Farrow Design is an award-winning consultancy set up by Mark Farrow. Farrow has worked with clients such as restaurateur Oliver Peyton, furniture retailer SCP and the Science Museum, London, and is well known for his continuing association with the Pet Shop Boys.

The idea for this packaging was simple—to pack an album release of the group Spiritualized like a box of pills, whether a single CD (or pill), or a course of 12 in the case of the special edition. The materials were not complicated, but success hinged on the investigation, sourcing and supply of a thermoformable tray that could be sealed with the printed foil material, exactly like a typical pharmaceutical product.

The packaging broke down into key areas: the carton, leaflet, tray and foil lid. The outer carton was made from a folding boxboard material that had been printed lithographically. It was simply a matter of establishing the weight and the bulk of this material, and increasing these slightly to compensate for the dimensions of a CD. The construction of this type of carton involves only one gluing. It also has flaps and tabs that can disintegrate very quickly. The construction was therefore modified slightly to ensure greater longevity.

The information leaflet is printed on a lightweight uncoated bond paper. It was found that most such leaflets are printed in incredibly high volumes via the web-printing method that is used to print newspapers. It was not possible to print these particular paper stocks, so an alternative sheet stock had to be sourced that approximated to the bulk and also gave the required level of show-through for the printed text. This leaflet then had to be folded at a specialist leaflet-folding company.

For the tray, it was found that the majority of pills are packed in either a clear or white PVC substrate. This is a fairly lightweight material and, like the carton, it had to be increased in bulk to compensate for the larger dimensions. A manufacturing company that produced this type of packaging was thus sourced—its selection was key to the authenticity of the packaging. Thermoforming has a very wide range of uses, and companies are set up to service certain specific business sectors—contacts in the field of pharmaceuticals proved vital for this key component that sealed the CDs in their packaging.

The world of drugs is very shadowy and secretive. The name of the drug always appears on the foil material and is the last thing to be both printed and supplied. It was important to check the quality of the printing process on the material and it proved very difficult to get samples when a multi-coloured logo was being considered. This resulted in a temporary slowdown in the development of the packaging, and written assurances had to be obtained to confirm that the designer was not working for a rival drug company.

A conventionally printed label had been considered for the reverse of the box. However, it was found that the technology and labelling systems used in pharmacies could be used and a visit to a chemist yielded details for the firm that supplied the machinery and services, and who were then employed to print all the labels.

There were few production problems, although the white PVC material being used for the thermoforming had to be shifted over to clear during the run, which makes certain versions of both the special and the normal release more collectible. Such an appropriation of manufacturing methods not normally associated with one particular type of packaging has probably never been so thoroughly explored. Every aspect of the process by which pharmaceutical pills are packed has been considered, sourced and utilized. Great foresight is required on the part of the designer and team to achieve such a fusion of idea, process and production—if successful the concept cannot later be replicated without appearing to be a facsimile of the original.

Materials
Werk No.12: Newsprint
Werk No.13: Newsprint, Paper (Coated)

Processes
Werk No.12: Binding, Hand Finishing, Lithography, Spray Painting
Werk No.13: Binding, Die Cutting, Hand Finishing, Lithography

WERK NO.12 GUERRILLAZINE 3. THE OUTSIDERS; WERK NO.13 JAN DE COCK
WORK

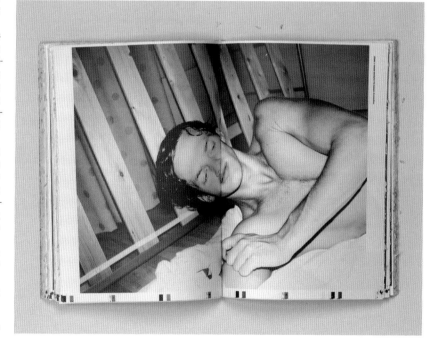

Established in 1996 by Theseus Chan, Work is a Singapore-based agency operating in the fields of advertising, fashion and publishing. *Werk* is a bi-annual magazine produced by Work in loose collaboration with the Japanese clothing label Comme des Garçons. Every issue starts from where the previous issue left off. There is no pre-conceived idea as to the content or form of each issue, or any notion of how it is to be printed and bound. Its uniqueness is achieved by the designers' constant striving to attain perfection through imperfections.

There are four different colour variants of *Werk No.12*. Each has been sprayed with fluorescent paint by a car-painting specialist. This process creates a powdery residue on the newsprint surface. Each cover has been hand torn, a method employed on previous issues, and then individually shrink-wrapped. Pages are left deliberately frayed at the edges.

Werk No.13 took its visual cues from the Belgian artist Jan De Cock. De Cock creates large-scale installations in response to the architecture of the site he is working in. *Werk No.13* documents one such installation created at Tate Modern, London. Built mainly from green plywood, its distinctive wood grain is mimicked in the side elevation of *Werk No.13*. The die cutting through the issue was used to echo the complexity of De Cock's work. Newsprint was used, with the inclusion of an alternating coated stock again echoing the plywood used in the artist's installation. The contrast between the surface textures, bulk and opacity of the two stocks once more reinforces facets of De Cock's work. The alignment of the die cuts is crucial to the concept of this issue. The die cuts are calculated to work with the images of the installations and add to their complexity. This careful positioning could not be done by machine, thus had to be achieved manually.

Werk is an impressive publication and an endless source of inspiration to designers. The printing and finishing techniques employed are frequently known only to the creators and, therefore, while relatively simple to them, seem highly complicated to the uninitiated.

jan de cock

WERK No.13

Spring/Summer 2006

Recorded and photographed by
Kirby Koh at the Tate Modern in London

WERK No.13: JAN DE COCK SPRING/SUMMER 2006

INDEX / PRINT

Daniel Mason is a writer and specialist in printing and packaging techniques. As the company Something Else, he continues to consult, source and produce innovative projects for the world's leading graphic designers and design groups, facilitating creativity with material and process.

Previous books include *Experimental Packaging* and *Limited Edition!?*, as well as monographs on Big Active, Blue Source, Tomato, Tom Hingston and Warren du Preez & Nick Thornton-Jones, and on Julie Verhoeven for the Japanese Gas Book series. He also researched the book *Designed by Peter Saville* along with being a regular contributor to *Atmosphere* magazine.

Something Else is based in London.

ACKNOWLEDGEMENTS

I would like to thank all of the designers, artists and individuals who have supported this project or lent their work, especially Nicholas Arpino, Mathias Augustyniak, Stefanie Barth, Vijay Bhudia, Kenneth A. Blake, Tim Bryans, Andrew Bunney, Tina Canais, Janis Church, Arnaud Delcolle, Mick Doherty, Brian Donnelly, Erica Donovan, Mark Farrow, Patricia Finegan, Albert Folch, Peter Frewer, Jens Grede, Jon Greig, Jiminie Ha, Toru Hachiga, Rob Hadrill, Eric Hampson, George Handley, Christian Hotte, Ricky Humphrey, Denis Huxtable, Helena Ichbiah, David Ives, Mark Jenkins, Richard Johns, Trudie Johnson, Laura Jones, Jos van de Kasteele, Robyn Katkhuda, Stephen Kennedy, Derek Landragin, Martin Laurenz, Henry Lavelle, Caroline Lebar, Pierre-François Letué, Alan Lewis, Jo Lightfoot, Terry Lucas, Ileana Makri, Martin Maw, Hiroki Nakamura, Paul Neale, Yumiko Ohchi, Claire Potter, Benoit Robert, Stefan Sagmeister, Gez Saint, Jen Schooling, Geoff Simpson, Phil Sims, David Soughton, Paul Stanway, Cristabel Stewart, Paul Stolper, Erik Torstensson, Martyn Wall, Gary Waterston, Jeff White, Lorraine Wilton and Terry Worby.

I would also like to thank John Jervis for his tireless support and encouragement, Oliver Knight for his peerless design work and also Will Thom for the superb photography.

The Bible on p.13 is reproduced by permission of the Secretary to the Delegates of Oxford University Press.

The Universal invitation on p.55 is reproduced by kind permission of Studio Fury.

Finally I would like to dedicate this book to Chloe, Celia and Edward.